# THE PANIZZI

## 2002

# THE PANIZZI LECTURES
## 2002

# Decisions and Revisions
# in T. S. Eliot

CHRISTOPHER RICKS

THE BRITISH LIBRARY
AND
FABER & FABER

First published 2003 by
The British Library
96 Euston Road
London NW1 2DB

Cataloguing in Publication Data
A catalogue record for this title is
available from The British Library

ISBN 0 7123 4843 3

Typeset by Cambridge Photosetting Services
Printed in England by Henry Ling (Printers) Ltd,
Dorchester

# Contents

# Acknowledgments

It is an honour to have been invited to give the Panizzi Lectures (2002) at the British Library. This short book is a revision of them.

T.S. Eliot's letter to Paul Elmer More is from the Paul Elmer More Papers, Manuscript Division, Department of Rare Books and Special Collections, Princeton University Library; published with permission of the Princeton University Library.

Further gratitude is more than in order: to Donald Gallup, for *T.S.Eliot: A Bibliography* (1969), without which no such scholarly inquiry would be possible; to Faber and Faber, and the good offices of John Bodley; to Mrs T.S. Eliot, for permitting quotation, and such extensive quotation, too; and, above all, to the poet and critic himself, whose art proves ceaselessly rewarding.

# Preface

The difference between high talent and genius is often made manifest in revision. That the artist was not to prove entirely satisfied with that which is a great deal better than anything you or I could do: this is a mark of transcendent powers, such powers as may take the especial form that is the self-transcending. When what we are responding to is the first draft of someone's (someone else's) work, we may sometimes find ourselves – while in some danger of self-satisfaction – judging it by the terms of Gerard M. Hopkins's 'Parnassian':

> Great men, poets I mean, have each their own dialect as it were of Parnassian, formed generally as they go on writing, and at last, – this is the point to be marked, – they can see things in this Parnassian way and describe them in this Parnassian tongue, without further effort of inspiration.

That such an achievement is something less than the highest is clarified by Hopkins, who goes on:

> Now it is a mark of Parnassian that one could conceive oneself writing it if one were the poet. Do not say that *if* you were Shakespeare you can imagine yourself writing Hamlet, because that is just what I think you can*not* conceive.[1]

---

1 *Further Letters of Gerard Manley Hopkins*, ed. Claude Colleer Abbott (1938), 1956 edn, pp.216–7.

But often the Parnassian is there as the writer's initial thought, along lines of insufficient resistance, and it is only in the inspired move of revising that he or she enters fully into his or her own, or rather into the work's own. When we come down to it, you or I might have come up with the first version, the maker's first effort at making – but not then with what, to our surprise and to the writer's too, was subsequently made of it.

*Decisions and Revisions in T. S. Eliot* attends to one specific embodiment of Eliot's re-thinking: changes that he made after publication. Such revisions have a different standing from any made prior to publication, and they raise questions about reception, audience, and (pre-eminently) self-criticism. In Eliot, the revisions are often substantial and are always acutely of interest, for they incarnate a movement of mind even after he had given the work to the world. As a poet, Eliot is understood never to have been a post-publication reviser on the American scale of Walt Whitman or Robert Lowell, or on the expatriate-English scale of Robert Graves. This truth has unfortunately meant that such revisions as there are (infrequently) in the poems and frequently in the prose have not much been pondered as evidence of his art and thought. Moreover, there has been an unthinking assumption that revisions to discursive prose – literary criticism and the like – do not, in the nature of the case, much matter. Yet to look at the cases is to see how much each may contain.

The opening section of *Decisions and Revisions in T. S. Eliot* is on Eliot's way with openings; the middle section, on his re-thinking of the middle matter; and the section that ends, on his revised decisions as to how to end.

Everything is initially made trickier by there being no scholarly edition of any of Eliot's prose works other than *The Varieties of Metaphysical Poetry* (the Clark Lectures that he delivered in 1926 and declined to publish), panoptically edited in 1993 by Ronald Schuchard. The anomalous situation is therefore that, as with *The Waste Land Manuscript*, edited with succinct aptness by Valerie Eliot in 1971, and as with the fifty early poems published in 1996 as *Inventions of the March Hare: Poems 1909-1917*, Eliot's *un*published work has been complemented by its textual variants and by its contextual settings in a way that none of his published work has been:

with editorial fullness. Only an editor would think that these provisions constitute nothing but gain (as though there were not always the danger of gratuitous intervenings), but an apparatus criticus need not harden into the pedantry petrified in *The Dunciad*, and the provider of such an apparatus is not necessarily an apparatchic.

Two studies of post-publication revision, on the rights and wrongs of such revision, are of exceptional wisdom and learning: Philip Horne, *Henry James and Revision* (1990), and George Hoffmann, *Montaigne's Career* (1998).

Since the Panizzi Lectures at The British Library have the happy duty of honouring the 'Prince of Librarians', Antonio Panizzi, it comes agreeably to hand that Panizzi's own career owed something to what it is to revise:

> In 1832, the Royal Society had come to the conclusion that a class or subject catalogue of the books in their library which had been lately compiled by one of their own members, should be revised and, if necessary, seen through the press by some more experienced cataloguer. In October, a Committee of the Council approved a suggestion that Panizzi should be approached and asked whether he would be willing to undertake this task. . .[2]

When we show ourselves willing to undertake a task, a show of modesty is often in order. The printed page may call for one form of the modesty topos, whereas the podium may call for another – there in the flesh, the lecturer may need to intimate a blush while taking care to eschew the simper or the *moue*. Tact is called for, called upon. Just how delicate these matters may be can be seen in both the accomplishment and the risks alive in what are likely to prove the best Panizzi Lectures that will ever be given: the very first, those delivered by D. F. McKenzie in 1985, *Bibliography and the Sociology of Texts*[3].

Rather as there has never been so extraordinary an inauguration as that which Eliot achieved with 'The Love Song of J. Alfred Prufrock' (is there any competitor at all to this, as the first poem in

2 Panizzi proved ready, willing, and all too able. Edward Miller, *Prince of Librarians: The Life and Times of Antonio Panizzi of the British Museum* (1967), p.85.
3 Published by The British Library, 1986; second edition, Cambridge University Press, 1999.

a poet's first book of poems?), so — even when one allows for the smaller scale of the valuable enterprise — there can seldom if ever have been a lecture-series that was initiated with richer substantiated speculation than this by D. F. McKenzie. So to select *Bibliography and the Sociology of Texts* itself as briefly the object of scrutiny when it comes to a lecturer's presentation of self in everyday life, and to mention its author's own acts of revision (which have some relation to bibliography and to sociology), may be to show something about the nature of occasions, and about how they inform, though they need not inform against, the thinking that they conduct.

As originally published by The British Library (though not in the later edition, by Cambridge University Press), *Bibliography and the Sociology of Texts* was explicit, in its opening words, as to differences of kind and of medium, in relation to certain forms of responsibility and their attendant modesties:

> These lectures were conceived and prepared, not as a text destined for print, but as lecture occasions.[4]

Those words all vanished in post-publication revision, one of them a large word, 'destined', pitched against the small claim of 'occasions'. Not but what you may suspect that, from the start, the lecturer really knew that in due course he was to submit to the Library a text for printing, even while he needed, as one always does on these occasions, to balance the readers' future claims against those of the present listeners, with the lecture as not just a genre but a medium.[5]

Some of McKenzie's claims were to find themselves evacuated, others fortified. Compare the foreword of 1986 with what replaced it in 1999.

> 1986: The challenge, as I saw it, was to sketch an extended role for bibliography at a time when traditional book forms must share with many new media their prime function of recording and transmitting texts.[6]

4 Foreword, p.ix.
5 See 'The Lecture' in Erving Goffman, *Forms of Talk* (1981), which is alert to the comedy of one's being engaged in reading, not hearing, its thinking.
6 The second sentence of the foreword.

1999: The familiar historical processes by which, over the centuries, texts have changed their form and content have now accelerated to a degree which makes the definition and location of textual authority barely possible in the old style.

Here, the opening sentence of the book has now accelerated to a degree which makes the location of the true text difficult, even while 'barely possible' leaves itself room (though barely) for manoeuvre even at this new speed. The changes that McKenzie makes, post-publication changes, are mostly bent upon pumping up his volume. In the original foreword, we had not been told four-squarely that the relationships between text and society 'preclude certain forms of discourse' and 'determine the very conditions under which meanings are created'. The lecture occasions had, it seems, asked a milder or a lesser assurance, even as they had asked for explicit modesty. As originally put:

> Redirecting bibliographical inquiry in a fruitful response to recent developments in critical theory and practice is certainly not easy, and in the succeeding text it is the challenge least adequately met.[7]

As genretically modified, the concession that is the last dozen words is no longer to be met with. For to end with 'not easy' is more easily said and done.

One form that post-publication revision may take is translation, particularly when it is authorized, the author at one with the translator.[8] Roger Chartier in 1991 (midway between the first and the second editions of *Bibliography and the Sociology of Texts*) set himself to up the ante, in the interests of the urgent burgeoner, *l'histoire du livre*. So McKenzie's original wording in the foreword, 'The partial but *significant shift* it signals is one from . . .', becomes 'Ce changement, bien qu'encore partiel, dénote une *modification profonde* . . .'

7 Foreword, p.x.
8 McKenzie, in his foreword to the second edition (1999): 'I owe a very special debt to Roger Chartier for giving the book a much wider circulation in French than it has hitherto received in English, and for his highly perspicacious preface to that edition'.

(my old italics, but Chartier's new emphasis). Likewise, the original phrasing, 'literary history and scholarship no longer look *quite as they did*', no longer looks quite as it did, and is indeed indisputably changed: '. . . ont *indiscutablement changé*'. The claims of the original text are systematically edited into unmisgivingness, with 'Each version *has some claim* to be edited in its own right' becoming 'Chaque version *mérite* d'être éditée . . .'.

McKenzie's book merited something a great deal better than this editing, though once the collaboration had started, there had always been the risk of reciprocated fervour. McKenzie praises, within Chartier's translation of his book, 'la magistrale *Histoire de l'édition française* dirigée par Henry-Jean Martin et Roger Chartier. Cette oeuvre majeure a déjà contribué . . .'. Historians of the book can turn out to be like any other historians. One good churn deserves another.

> While ladling butter from alternate tubs
> Stubbs butters Freeman, Freeman butters Stubbs.

Stubbs' Charters, McKenzie's Chartier.

# In the Beginning

Eliot was preoccupied with second thoughts, as in the notable act of re-thinking that is 'Second Thoughts about Humanism'[9]. One complication elsewhere within Eliot's second thoughts may derive from the fact that so much of his early thinking was published anonymously, and there is something teasing about the thought of a thinker's second thoughts when you are not sure who he or she was in the first thinking place. Eliot must be among the few great critics, himself the greatest of them, to have published much of his greatest work anonymously.[10] If Eliot's *Selected Essays* were to lack the dozen thoroughgoing contributions to the *Times Literary Supplement*, although it would still be an unignorable achievement it would be a drastically attenuated one in comparison with what his indebtedness to Bruce Richmond fostered by way of our debt to them both.

It was in one such anonymous review, of F.H. Bradley's *Ethical*

---

9  1929. The title was revised from 'Second Thoughts on Humanism' (*New Adelphi*, June/August 1929). It follows upon 'The Humanism of Irving Babbitt', a year earlier.

10  On anonymity, see Anne Ferry, '*Anonymity*: the Literary History of a Word' (*New Literary History*, Spring 2002), with its lucid anatomy: '*Anonymous*: Its Root Meaning', '*Anonymity*: An Aesthetic Ideal', '*Anonymity*: A Cultural Motif', and '*Anonymity*: A Modernist Paradox', on Eliot and Wordsworth.

*Studies* (1927), that Eliot put his mind to what it is to change one's mind, or to seldom have to:

> The unity of Bradley's thought is not the unity attained by a man who never changes his mind. If he had so little occasion to change it, that is because he usually saw his problems from the beginning in all their complexity and connexions – saw them, in other words, with wisdom – and because he could never be deceived by his own metaphors – which, indeed, he used most sparingly – and was never tempted to make use of current nostrums.[11]

How slyly *his own metaphors* proceeds towards *nostrums*, a nostrum being our own.

For Eliot, the creative dissatisfaction that marks the enduring artist may often be evidenced in the pertinacity of second thoughts, and of third if need be.[12]

In a letter to the Editor of the *Times Literary Supplement* (3 November 1921), Eliot – subscribing himself 'your obliged humble CONTRIBUTOR') – contested George Sainsbury's generalization about the Caroline poets.

> The 'second thoughts' to which he alludes are, I think, and as I tried to point out, frequent in the work of many other poets besides, of other times and other languages. I have mentioned Chapman, and the contemporaries of Dante. I do not believe that the author of *Hamlet* and *Measure for Measure* was invariably satisfied with 'the first simple, obvious, natural thought and expression of thought'; or that the author of the 'Phoenix and Turtle' whistled as he went for want of thought. Nor can I believe that Swinburne thought twice, or even *once*, before he wrote

11  *Selected Essays* (1932), 1951 edition, p.453. Cited hereafter as *Selected Essays*. Compare Eliot in his (later, and signed) obituary of John Maynard Keynes, *New English Weekly* (16 May 1946): 'it is evident that he had the free mind which is not afraid to change'.

12  On the related matter of the borrowing by writers from themselves, remarked by Eliot, see Eliot, *Inventions of the March Hare: Poems 1909–1917*, ed. Christopher Ricks (1996), Appendix D (iii). Such self-borrowing is a form of revision, sometimes post-publication.

> Time with a gift of tears,
> Grief with a glass that ran.[13]

The saunter of this (no trudging along, here), even while it deprecates the blitheness of a certain critical mentality, is visible in the move from *went* to *ran*, just as it is audible in the allusions. First, that to Dryden:

> He trudg'd along unknowing what he sought,
> And whistled as he went, for want of Thought.
> (*Cymon and Iphigenia* 84–5)

There is a good and a bad side to the thought 'unknowing what he sought' (for some such lack of self-consciousness may be valuable to the artist, even while there is no substitute for thought or – on occasion – for second thoughts). And why, of all poems, 'The Phoenix and Turtle'? Perhaps because the poem, a metaphysical union of the one and the many, is a supreme imagining of two becoming one. Rather as second thoughts may be not the repudiation but the consummation of what had been initiated.

> So they loved as love in twaine,
> Had the essence but in one,
> Two distincts, Division none,
> Number there in love was slaine.

> Single Natures double name,
> Neither two nor one was called.

> That it cried, how true a twaine,
> Seemeth this concordant one,

– this, as conceiving not only of second thoughts as a true twain, a concordant one (atonement, at-one-ment), but of allusion as an imaginative form of second thoughts, itself revising or revisionary.

13 *The Letters of T.S. Eliot: volume 1 1898–1922*, ed. Valerie Eliot (1988), p.483.

Second thoughts as revised judgments are a strength in Eliot's criticism, even while they may sometimes puzzle or thwart. The case of George Herbert remains – within the criticism, though not in the indebted art of *Four Quartets* – something of a perplexity. In 'Religion and Literature' (1935), Eliot had set particular limits to his claims for Herbert when it comes to such curtailed poetry as is 'the product of a special religious awareness, which may exist without the general awareness which we expect of the major poet':

> I do not pretend to offer Vaughan, or Southwell, or George Herbert, or Hopkins as major poets: I feel sure that the first three, at least, are poets of this limited awareness.[14]

'I feel sure. . .' But this or such was not Eliot's way. He thinks again, especially about what he feels, and in 'What is Minor Poetry?' (1944) he comes to judge differently: 'So in the end, I, for one, cannot admit that Herbert can be called a "minor" poet'.[15] But then, as often happens, 'in the end' declines to be conclusive, and five years later, Eliot finds himself again obliged to judge anew, and – in doing so – to judge his own critical movements of mind, moved (in the words of a telling title of his) to criticize the critic. Dated 1949, four lines are added at the foot of a page of 'Religion and Literature', drily casting the words 'I note' as a note:

> I note that in an address delivered in Swansea some years later (subsequently published in *The Welsh Review* under the title of 'What Is Minor Poetry?') I stated with some emphasis my opinion that Herbert is a major, not a minor poet. I agree with my later opinion.

Well, to say (as Eliot had done in 1944) that you 'cannot admit that Herbert can be called a "minor" poet' is scarcely the same as stating with some emphasis your opinion that Herbert is a major not a minor poet. Something remains dark in all this, even while there is a bright edge to the final asseveration, 'I agree with my later opinion'.

---

14 *Selected Essays*, p.391. Phrases cognate with 'I do not pretend' thread their way through Eliot's engagements of this kind.
15 *On Poetry and Poets* (1957), p.46.

Eliot as a critic is characterized not only by having been repeatedly moved to a later opinion, self-impelled to judge anew his own judgments as to some of the greatest writers, but also by openly discussing and pondering this process itself. Of these, the famous or notorious case is Milton, in two pieces that Eliot came to dub laconically 'Milton I' (originally 'A Note on the Verse of John Milton', 1936) and 'Milton II' (originally 'Milton', 1947). Both were to remain in print (in *On Poetry and Poets*), and they even came to constitute a paperback duo or duet,[16] with the later essay overtly discussing these second thoughts while covertly discarding most of the evidence that had been instanced, and the attendant argumentation.[17]

Less inflammatory, more sage, is the essay on 'Goethe as the Sage' (1955), half of which is on second thoughts, specifically on self-criticism, even attuned to the Tennysonian trinity, 'Self-reverence,

16 *Milton: Two Studies* (1968).
17 Four or five pages were omitted (pp.14–18 of the original lecture), pages that began: 'I now come to the point at which it is desirable to quote passages in illustration of what I have been saying about Milton's versification'. It had apparently ceased to be desirable. A pity, because all the critical life was in the engagement with the instances, an engagement that was not, in my judgment, persuasive in the end (see my book, *Milton's Grand Style*, 1963) but that remains valuably provocative. After this large and silent omission, Eliot took up his concluding thoughts: 'I come at last to compare my own attitude, as that of a poetical practitioner perhaps typical of a generation twenty-five years ago, with my attitude today.... I wished to make clear those excellences of Milton which particularly impress me, before explaining why I think that the study of his verse might at last be of benefit to poets' (*On Poetry and Poets*, p.159). But this does not really happen, once the instances are dropped. F.R. Leavis was indignant: 'The impulse it represents is so radical that the surrender, the connivance, need not be fully conscious. Yet, reading the British Academy lecture on Milton (reprinted in this volume with, I see when I compare it with the reply that I – not, of course, challenged there by any actual mention of my name – made to the original, some unsignalled and very substantial omissions),★ who can believe that the writer and lecturer could have been unaware of the felicity of touch, the tactics, the strategy, the phrasing, the whole thing, for the reassurance and ingratiation of a British Academy public?'
    ★ [footnote] '"Each item is substantially the same as on the date of its delivery or first publication." – T.S.Eliot, Preface. This one isn't'. ('T.S.Eliot as Critic', *The Common Pursuit*, 1952, p.189.)

self-knowledge, self-control'. Eliot knew the charge that he risked (not courted): 'It may seem egotistic frivolity for me to spend so much time on the mutations of my own attitude towards Goethe.'[18] Yet far from being egotistic or frivolous, the re-thinking is an occasion for self-criticism of a kind that is touching and chastening. Many are the cases that Eliot revisited in some such spirit: Donne, of whom he came to think and feel less well; Tennyson, and Yeats, the reverse; Henry James, who goes quietly.

Yet there is a tacit surprise here: Eliot's lack of interest, it would seem, in the practice of revision itself within the work of these and other writers. He attends to many who are characterized by revising greatly after publication, and yet there is, for instance, nothing said about Yeats's revision within Eliot's late tribute, despite everything that Eliot remarks as to Yeats early and late. Again, his thinking about Tennyson makes nothing of Tennyson the reviser, and the same goes for Henry James, and for Wordsworth and Coleridge.

It is odd, and distinctly memorable, that it should be in the Yeats lecture – Yeats the indefatigable re-reader of his own work – that Eliot should speak as he does:

> It may be that I expressed myself badly, or that I had only an adolescent grasp of that idea – as I can never bear to re-read my own prose writings, I am willing to leave the point unsettled – but I think now, at least, that the truth of the matter is as follows . . .[19]

Yet how else, other than with the help of re-reading, could he possibly have revised so many of them, as he did?

As a poet, Eliot is characterized by not much having second thoughts – after publication – about the exact wording of his poems. There are few instances of post-publication revision, as against the entire intensity of revision prior to publication, and such instances as do exist will be found to be mostly prior to the

18 *On Poetry and Poets*, p.210.
19 *On Poetry and Poets*, p.255. Compare 'The Music of Poetry' (1942): 'I can never re-read any of my own prose writings without acute embarrassment: I shirk the task, and consequently may not take account of all the assertions to which I have at one time or another committed myself' (*On Poetry and Poets*, p.26).

collecting of a poem within a volume. In 1926, he said: 'My attitude is that of a craftsman who has attempted for eighteen years to make English verses, studying the work of dead artisans who have made better verses.'[20] Making his own verses better was an extraordinary process that ordinarily came to an end with publication. Having long tailored, he did not tinker.

(Meanwhile it remains one of life's little ironies that Eliot, who was not only a publisher for so much of his life but was for most of his work his own publisher, should never have been able to precipitate an entirely dependable text of the poems.)

To begin with a small beginning: there is in the *Selected Essays* a much-vexed essay called HAMLET (the house-style for all the essays: capitals, roman, intimating here, perhaps, not the play but the character).[21] Elsewhere, there is in *The Sacred Wood*, a book which has been in print since 1920, alongside *Selected Essays* since 1932, an essay called 'Hamlet and His Problems' (1919). This both is and is not the same essay. Texts and Their Problems.[22] For in *The Sacred Wood*, 'Hamlet and His Problems' begins: 'Few critics have even admitted that *Hamlet* the play is the primary problem, and Hamlet the character only secondary'. Whereas HAMLET begins: 'Few critics have ever admitted [. . .]'

I admit that 'even admitted' and 'ever admitted' both make (different) sense. I do not myself believe that Eliot actively chose to keep the variant alive; it has survived to this day with its independent tenacity.[23] But Eliot certainly chose to kill, there in

---

20  *The Varieties of Metaphysical Poetry*, p.44.

21  The book reviewed by 'T.S.E.' in the *Athenaeum* (26 September 1919) was called *The Problem of "Hamlet"*; no problem there as to whether the play or the character is meant, any more than there is with what had been Eliot's title there: 'Hamlet and His Problems'.

22  The philosopher David Wiggins renewed not a copyright but an argument in his *Sameness and Substance Renewed* (2001). The preface (p.ix) is strikingly pre-emptive: 'Whether *Sameness and Substance Renewed* is the same book as *Sameness and Sustance* [1980] is not a question of importance – the matter of a joke that will fail nobody who wants to make it, or else of an exercise for the reader'. But a good joke hereabouts would exercise a reader's wits, and might not be without importance.

23  In 1997, as published by Faber (retrieved at last from Methuen), *The Sacred Wood* preserves 'Few critics have even admitted...'

*The Sacred Wood*, the opening of what had been the original text, as published in the *Athenaeum* (26 September 1919):

> We are glad to find Hamlet in the hands of so learned and scrupulous a critic as Mr Robertson. Few critics have even admitted that *Hamlet* the play is the primary problem, and Hamlet the character only secondary.

By the next year, a book review had become an essay. The excision then makes sense, but it also changes the sense's movement. When Eliot dropped the opening sentence of the original review, he changed the ensuing intonation, and thereby modified the impulse and the meaning to some oblique degree. 'Few critics have ever . . .' (or 'have even . . .'): this vaults into action. 'We are glad to find Hamlet in the hands of so learned and scrupulous a critic as Mr Robertson': this had sidled in, with its own gestures of the hands. Neither version is to be preferred, nor should the two be assimilated. But you do say or hear the word 'critics' differently if you have just heard tell of a particular 'critic'. So although it would be an exaggeration to say that there is all the difference in the world, there is some difference in the world of animus between a syntax that sets 'so learned and scrupulous a critic as Mr Robertson' against the immediately succeeding words, 'Few critics have . . .', and a syntax that begins not with a cautious entrance but with despatch and by despatching.

The nub is occasion, and yet the instance (which ought to be uncomplicated, a book review, after all) has its elusiveness. What exactly is going on is difficult, perhaps impossible, to say.

Eliot was often keen to say something about occasions and how they affect the gathering-up of essays and talks into books. His preface to *On Poetry and Poets* engages directly the points of protocol and of courtesy, as well as of format and medium:

> Of the sixteen essays which make up the present book, ten were originally addressed directly to audiences; an eleventh essay, that on Virgil, was a broadcast talk. In publishing these addresses now, I have not attempted to transform them into what they might have been if originally designed for the eye instead of the ear; nor have I made alterations beyond omitting the prefatory

remarks to *Poetry and Drama*, and also some of those preambular remarks and incidental pleasantries which, having been intended to seduce the listener, might merely irritate the reader.

The modesty topos finds itself duly, not inordinately, called upon: 'seduce' is itself a seductive admission, and 'preambular' is discreet of gait. But all the same, there is some danger of our acceding too equably to the claim, made in all or more than all modesty, that the prefatory and the preambular and the incidental have been excised without any real loss. I shall argue that Eliot's preambular remarks characteristically have a distinctly illuminating relation to the body of what follows. This is a good thing, but it does mean that – even in cases when the move from the spoken word to the words on the page was rightly judged to necessitate some omissions – a price is having to be paid. Eliot was always a great one for insisting, unsentimentally and often ruefully, that to enjoy such-and-such is to be precluded from enjoying so-and-so. He has excellent judgment when it comes to seeing the ways in which (given a change of occasion, with listeners now becoming readers) certain things will have to go. But since he had exercised his preambulations wisely in the original circumstances, it will not do to avert our eyes from the sacrifices that are now being made.

For what would it be for Eliot's preambles to have failed, all along, to be integral to the argument that follows them? And when, because of the change of medium, the preambles need to go, how can this not involve some forfeiting, not of integrity, but of the integral?

In his preface to *On Poetry and Poets*, Eliot mentions, as one instance, his omitting the prefatory remarks to *Poetry and Drama*. What is sacrificed, rightly but sadly, is a moving account of Theodore Spencer, in whose name the particular series of Harvard lectures had been founded. As reprinted in *On Poetry and Poets*, the lecture that has now become an essay pays its tribute to Theodore Spencer only in the form of a formal footnote as to 'The first Theodore Spencer Memorial Lecture . . .'. As earlier published in England as a slim volume, *Poetry and Drama* had opened with three pages (in italics, to differentiate the nature of their enterprise) poignantly evoking Spencer. As originally published by Harvard

University Press, six months earlier in 1951, the body of the text had been preceded by a fuller description of, and tribute to, Spencer's doings and achievements at Harvard. This had called up and called upon local affections:

> If I speak of him at greater length than is usual on such occasions, I feel sure that you will not only excuse but approve my doing so. There must be many of his friends and former pupils in this audience; much that I shall say of him will therefore be familiar knowledge; but I am sure that an act of homage to his personality, his work, and his influence will be welcome to all of you.

The greater length was later curtailed. Eliot was right to judge any such localizing to be inappropriate to the different undertaking that is *On Poetry and Poets*. What matters has become not an act of homage in itself but a revised decorum. Decorum asks a due modesty. Eliot speaks openly about his long engagement with poetry and drama[24]:

> Reviewing my critical output for the last thirty-odd years, I am surprised to find how constantly I have returned to the drama, whether by examining the work of the contemporaries of Shakespeare, or by reflecting on the possibilities of the future. It may even be that people are weary of hearing me on this subject. But, while I find that I have been composing variations on this theme all my life, my views have been continually modified and renewed by increasing experience; so that I am impelled to take stock of the situation afresh at every stage of my own experimentation.

It is relevant to any such process of continually modifying and renewing and taking stock that this very paragraph should have found itself taken stock of and modified. The English edition came to end this, the first paragraph proper of the argument, with 'every stage of my own experimentation'. The American edition had gone

24 Gallup records, of the lecture: 'Based, in part, upon an earlier lecture, delivered to European audiences in 1949 and printed in the periodical *Adam* (November 1949) with title, "The Aims of Poetic Drama"'.

on: 'And I hope that I have profited by this experience'. A perfectly natural hope, but not one that, on second thoughts, it is possible to voice without sounding prim or 'umble.

These are matters of tone, than which few things are more important on these occasions. Matters of substance join matters of tone on another occasion when there was a particular audience attentive to drama, and when we should be sensitive to the sacrifice that revision, albeit justified, may then entail. The event was Eliot's address to the Shakespeare Association in 1927, issuing in one of his most challenging sequences of thought, 'Shakespeare and the Stoicism of Seneca'.

As uttered, and as first published at two shillings, it began with artful artistry. Those who do not like its manner will find it guilty of flimflam, flattery, and flummery. Others of us may relish the stealthy impudence of its propitiatory tissue, its mimic mockery of modesty, its subversive subservience. 'Desiring this man's gift and that man's scope': the line from *Ash-Wednesday* is overtly along the lines of Shakespeare's Sonnet 29: 'Desiring this man's art, and that man's scope'. Hear the scope of the opening:

> Desiring to make the most of the opportunity which had been given me of addressing the inmost circle of Shakespeare experts, I cast about, as any other mere journalist would do in the circumstances, for some subject in treating which I could best display my agility and conceal my ignorance of all the knowledge of which everyone present is master. I abandoned several interesting topics on which I might hope to impress almost any other audience – such as the development of dramatic blank verse or the relation of Shakespeare to Marlowe – in favour of one which, if I am in disagreement with anybody, I shall be in disagreement with persons whose opinions will be regarded as suspiciously by the Shakespeare Association as are my own. I am a timid person, easily overawed by authority; in what I have to say I hope that authority is at least as likely to be of my opinion as not.
>
> The last few years have witnessed a number of recrudescences of Shakespeare. [. . .]

As we have it in *Selected Essays*, 'Shakespeare and the Stoicism of Seneca' opens, in vigorous immediacy, with that last sentence: 'The last few years have witnessed a number of recrudescences of Shakespeare'. Swift and deft, and liking the sound as well as the thought of 'recrudescences'. But something of value did vanish when those preamblings were excised. For they have their own delicious disconcertings, these feints and velleities and stylizations, this speaking of 'Shakespeare experts' (as though an 'expert' in literature were not suspect to the point of indictment – and 'the inmost circle of Shakespeare experts'? Where exactly is the inmost circle of Dante experts going to end up?), its gravelling its listeners by affecting to grovel ('as any other mere journalist would do'), its speaking of how best to display not its ability but its 'agility', while not concealing its wish to 'conceal my ignorance of all the knowledge of which everyone present is master'. (What, *everyone*? This is masterly.) 'I am a timid person, easily overawed by authority' – but not, I can assure me, easily gulled by self-styled authorities, gullible though the 'experts' themselves are when it comes to such flattery as is laid on with a vengeance.[25]

Merely preambular remarks, these? Incidental pleasantries? But they are integral to a tone that distinguishes 'Shakespeare and the Stoicism of Seneca' from, for instance, an essay of the same year, 'Seneca in Elizabethan Translation'. For three paragraphs after this

25 As to experts, recall a passage from 'The Function of Criticism' (*The Criterion*, ii, October 1923, 35–6), revised by Eliot, that originally declared that 'the Catholic practitioners were, I believe, with the possible exception of heretical experts who were often Teutonic, not palpitating Narcissi; the Catholic did not believe that God and himself were identical'. This became, less palpitatingly, '... with the possible exception of certain heretics, not ...' (*Selected Essays*, p.27). As for the prejudicial *Teutonic*: Housman, in a talk published the previous year (1922), had scorned its ease: 'Patriotism has a great name as a virtue, and in civic matters, at the present stage of the world's history, it possibly still does more good than harm; but in the sphere of intellect it is an unmitigated nuisance. I do not know which cuts the worse figure: a German scholar encouraging his countrymen to believe that "wir Deutsche" have nothing to learn from foreigners, or an Englishman demonstrating the unity of Homer by sneers at "Teutonic professors," who are supposed by his audience to have goggle eyes behind large spectacles, and ragged moustaches saturated in lager beer, and consequently to be incapable of forming literary judgments'. ('The Application of Thought to Textual Criticism', *Housman: Collected Poems and Selected Prose*, ed. Christopher Ricks, 1988, p.328.)

excised preamble to 'Shakespeare and the Stoicism of Seneca', there is such an admission as this ('admit' being once more a word to reckon with in these turns of speech):

> I admit that my own experience, as a minor poet, may have jaundiced my outlook; that I am used to having cosmic significances, which I never suspected, extracted from my work (such as it is) by enthusiastic persons at a distance; and to being informed that something which I meant seriously is *vers de société*; and to having my personal biography reconstructed from passages which I got out of books, or which I invented out of nothing because they sounded well; and to having my biography invariably ignored in what I *did* write from personal experience; so that in consequence I am inclined to believe that people are mistaken about Shakespeare just in proportion to the relative superiority of Shakespeare to myself.[26]

This is at once deadly serious and itself *vers* or rather *prose de société*. It constitutes my personal favourite from Eliot's personal remarks, one sentence of a dozen lines, where modesty and majesty unite in a heartfelt and headfelt polemical irrefutability. It continues to work admirably within 'Shakespeare and the Stoicism of Seneca' as we still have it − and yet something was inevitably lost when, by the removal of the preamble that had been uttered by a *soi-disant* 'mere journalist', the later cognate sentence was given the responsibility for inaugurating the mocking modesty, instead of being a continuation of Eliot's initial politics by other means. The preambular remarks, after all, had been calculated to lead into not only the strategy but the tactics of the argument.

The scrupulosity of 'I am inclined to believe', with its inclination of the head; the deeper inclination of the head for 'my work (such as it is)' (Eliot, the master of the unplumbable parenthesis); the waiving of those poetical passages 'which I invented out of nothing because they sounded well' (how good this sounds, and how well the audience is being sounded); the doffing of such comparison as would be odious, 'in proportion to the relative superiority of Shakespeare to myself': these steely foilings had

26 *Selected Essays*, p.127.

flourished a differently penetrating precision when they had been anticipated (not pre-empted) by the original preamble. The experience of the original opening was germane to the subsequent experience that is being invoked here: 'I admit that my own experience, as a minor poet, may have jaundiced my outlook'. Mordant, this. (Oh! he is minor, is he? Then I wish that he would bite some other of my majors.)

I think of Herbert and the major/minor imbroglio, and I think of what it was for Eliot to have established within his *Collected Poems* a section headed 'Minor Poems'. At once modest and inestimably proud (like Beckett's title for his film: *Film*), 'Minor Poems' might be thought to be an intimation of something as to the standing of all the Eliot poems that escape such a heading. It was one thing for Tennyson to proffer, as his own categorising, 'Juvenilia', which set the great early poem 'Mariana' in the company of such feathery songs as the two to 'The Owl'. It is another thing for Eliot, un-owlish, to attribute minorness to certain of his poems. And very good poems, too, numbering, among the thirteen, the grave historic 'Landscapes' and the acute histrionic 'Lines for an Old Man'.

But there was a loss entailed when the preamble rightly went, and the loss goes beyond Eliot's maintenance of his searching way of speaking. For the core of his argument is itself anticipated by the preamble in which Eliot had staged himself to such effect in affect-ing the abashed or the bashful. At the heart of 'Shakespeare and the Stoicism of Seneca' is a proposition as to all such self-staging:

> Nevertheless, there is, in some of the great tragedies of Shakespeare, a new attitude. It is not the attitude of Seneca, but is derived from Seneca; it is slightly different from anything that can be found in French tragedy, in Corneille or in Racine; it is modern, and it culminates, if there is ever any culmination, in the attitude of Nietzsche. I cannot say that it is Shakespeare's 'philosophy'. Yet many people have lived by it; though it may only have been Shakespeare's instinctive recognition of something of theatrical utility. It is the attitude of self-dramatization assumed by some of Shakespeare's heroes at moments of tragic intensity.[27]

27 *Selected Essays*, p. 129. Eliot's acute angle was in some ways anticipated by that excellent Victorian critic Richard Holt Hutton, in 'Sayings of Great Men':

Other dramatists had practised this. 'But Shakespeare, of course, does it very much better than any of the others, and makes it somehow more integral with the human nature of his characters. It is less verbal, more real'. And so into the last great speech of Othello (which has its own assumption of the minimal and the modest, 'a word or two'): 'Soft you; a word or two before you go. . .' The climax: '. . . And smote him thus'. And thence into Eliot's indeflectible characterizing of Othello's true character and his false moves.

> What Othello seems to me to be doing in making this speech is *cheering himself up*. He is endeavouring to escape reality, he has ceased to think about Desdemona, and is thinking about himself. Humility is the most difficult of all virtues to achieve; nothing dies harder than the desire to think well of oneself. Othello succeeds in turning himself into a pathetic figure, by adopting an *aesthetic* rather than a moral attitude, dramatizing himself against his environment. He takes in the spectator, but the human motive is primarily to take in himself. I do not believe that any writer has ever exposed this *bovarysme*, the human will to see things as they are not, more clearly than Shakespeare.[28]

There is at once the compassionate and the dispassionate in the turn of phrase that, contemplating Othello on the brink of suicide, insists that 'nothing dies harder than the desire to think well of oneself'. There is the relative superiority of Shakespeare not only 'to myself' (as earlier), but to the great writer without whom we should never even have had the word *bovarysme*. 'I do not believe that any writer has ever exposed this *bovarysme*, the human will to see things as they

'Indeed, the essence of the grandest sayings appears to be that in such sayings the speaker flings down his glove to all the forces which are fighting against him, and deliberately regards himself as the champion in some dramatic conflict the centre of which he is. Cromwell's "Paint me as I am," and the more elaborate though not more memorable, "I have sought the Lord night and day that He would rather slay me than put me upon the doing of this work," or his reputed saying of Charles, "We will cut off his head with the crown on it," all implied his supreme conviction that he was the involuntary Minister of a great series of providential acts'. (Collected in *Brief Literary Criticisms*, 1906, p.26.)

28 *Selected Essays*, pp.130–1.

are not, more clearly than Shakespeare' – any writer, even Flaubert himself.

But Eliot's extraordinarily compelling reading of *Othello*, compelling even if resisted, is no longer exactly the same now that it figures without the lecture's original preamble. When Eliot says of Othello that 'He takes in the spectator, but the human motive is primarily to take in himself', we may find ourselves remembering Eliot's words elsewhere about his own self-presentation, and his having come to omit 'those preambular remarks and incidental pleasantries which, having been intended to seduce the listener, might merely irritate the reader'. What Eliot had seized as his original point of entry had been powerfully at one with his succeeding focus, 'Shakespeare's instinctive recognition of something of theatrical utility' – Shakespeare's recognition and Eliot's own, since the lecturer, the lecturer on drama, had proved skilled at availing himself of something of theatrical utility. For 'the attitude of self-dramatization assumed by some of Shakespeare's heroes at moments of tragic intensity' had been assumed by Eliot at his opening moment of unheroic comic intensity, when Eliot too, like Othello while so unlike him, had been 'dramatizing himself against his environment'. Self-dramatization within Shakespeare's plays was praised as 'more integral with the human nature of his characters'. Self-dramatization at the opening of Eliot's very lecture was integral with the human nature of Eliot's character.

The insight developed in 'Shakespeare and the Stoicism of Seneca' had been adumbrated in '"Rhetoric" and Poetic Drama' (1919), or, more precisely, in the revision of that essay[29] when it was collected in *The Sacred Wood* a year later. At that time, Eliot added some comments on Ben Jonson, saying of Sylla's ghost in *Catiline*, and of Envy in *The Poetaster*, that 'These two figures are contemplating their own dramatic importance, and quite properly'. In Shakespeare, too, he added, 'we have this necessary advantage of a new clue to the character, in noting the angle from which he views himself'. Which might bring us back to the opening moment there at the Shakespeare Association in 1927:

29 'Whether Rostand Had Something about Him', when it originally appeared in the *Athenaeum* (25 July 1919).

Desiring to make the most of the opportunity which had been given me of addressing the inmost circle of Shakespeare experts, I cast about, as any other mere journalist would do in the circumstances, for some subject in treating which I could best display my agility and conceal my ignorance of all the knowledge of which everyone present is master.

Noting the angle from which Eliot viewed himself, we were able to make the most of the opportunity to contemplate a figure contemplating his own dramatic importance, and quite properly – that is, without self-importance, since a certain kind of discomfiture, felt as well as inflicted, was on this occasion so fitting.

My proposition, then, is a simple one, although Eliot's embodiment of the principle was not simple since it asked the utmost tact of him, and asked furthermore that he be willing to sacrifice those initiatory accomplishments that were much more than incidental pleasantries since they had a supple and subtle part to play in advancing the arguments to come.

The accomplishment on the occasion of 'Shakespeare and the Stoicism of Seneca', its skill of *address*, may be seen the more clearly if we contrast its pertinence of pleasantry with another occasion, six years later, when Eliot was again obliged to issue some prefatory disclaimers but proved less happy in the disowning and the disarming. This time the occasion was not scholastic and literary but theological and religious: 'Catholicism and International Order: Opening Address to the Anglo-Catholic Summer School of Sociology' (September 1933).[30]

Eliot's opening address opened with a paragraph that was to be excised when, three years later, the spoken words that hymned Catholicism became an essay ancient and modern:[31]

This is by no means the first occasion on which I have had to speak in public on a subject outside of my competence. I appear first as a speaker at a session during which you will hold

30 *Christendom* (September 1933); collected in *Essays Ancient and Modern* (1936), but not reprinted by Eliot thereafter.
31 *Essays Ancient and Modern.* The printing in *Christendom*, in the month when the address was delivered, had retained this opening paragraph, just as had done the separate publication of 'Shakespeare and the Stoicism of Seneca'.

discussions with men who, to say nothing of their greater abilities than mine, have acquired the special knowledge, and devoted the special thinking, which qualifies them for the task; and I ought to be here only as an inconspicuous auditor. There are, of course, public men for whose opinions on *any* subject there is always a large and interested audience. I have no desire to join this popular profession; I suspect that their public is often animated rather by vulgar curiosity, or the anticipation of a lark, than by a serious craving for self-improvement; and the speaker, in such circumstances, is liable to descend to the rôle of a mere Entertainer. I must, therefore, try to present and keep fixed in your minds the concept of the common man: in other words, introduce myself as the highly intelligent ignoramus who hopes to be able to express his confusion with clarity, and ask the right questions which will be answered by others more competent.

I assume that we are all of one mind about the deplorable consequences of the schisms of Christianity, and are convinced of the vital importance of the reunion of Christendom.

On the straight face of it, the self-deprecation and self-depreciation here may not seem so different from those that met the Shakespeare Association. The reference, twice, to an insufficient competence, the acknowledgment that others have 'their greater abilities' (not agility): these are not launched only to 'seduce' the listeners, but they will need to be on their guard if they are not to be construed as not so much playful as ployful. And the movement does slip, I believe, at a few points.

'I ought to be here only as an inconspicuous auditor': T. S. Eliot may quite like the thought of an inconspicuous auditorship but he knows his audience, and he knows that it is an audience for whom he, in 1933, could not be inconspicuous. (After all, or before all, his conspicuousness had, rightly, contributed to his being invited to give this opening address.) Some of his moves are too patently slides, as when the declaration that 'I must, therefore, try to present and keep fixed in your minds the concept of the common man' is immediately followed by 'in other words', and this when it is not only the words that are other but the thought itself:

. . . the concept of the common man: in other words, introduce myself as the highly intelligent ignoramus who hopes to be able to express his confusion with clarity, and ask the right questions which will be answered by others more competent.

The common man may be an ignoramus, but Eliot is not, and he and his audience know so, which means that for Eliot to 'introduce' himself as such is an inordinate feint. For Eliot was manifestly the legendary speaker who needs no introduction, least of all this one. And 'the common man' may be an ignoramus, but is not − least of all for Eliot − 'highly intelligent'.

In the address to the Shakespeare Association, it had been well understood what it was for Eliot to speak of his casting about,

> as any other mere journalist would do in the circumstances, for some subject in treating which I could best display my agility and conceal my ignorance of all the knowledge of which everyone present is master.

But the casting about, in serious comedy, as to how to conceal his ignorance is very different from his casting himself as an ignoramus, even a highly intelligent one. And the word 'mere' had enjoyed a very different role back then. 'As any other mere journalist would do': this kept many necessary forms of animus in play. But the Anglo-Catholic Summer School of Sociology asked a different story. Animus of some sort was still called for, lest the occasion become too bland for words. Catholicism, including Anglo-Catholicism, was in danger, and the serious discussion of these matters was − as Eliot sharply said − threatened by those professional pontificators from whom he needed to dissociate his sensibility:

> There are, of course, public men for whose opinions on *any* subject there is always a large and interested audience. I have no desire to join this popular profession; I suspect that their public is often animated rather by vulgar curiosity, or the anticipation of a lark, than by a serious craving for self-improvement; and the speaker, in such circumstances, is liable to descend to the rôle of a mere Entertainer.

A palpable hit. But perhaps too palpably a hit. 'A mere journalist' had not beaten its breast but it had not beaten anybody else's breast either, whereas 'to descend to the rôle of a mere Entertainer' does, rather. It descends to name-calling, and descends the more when it elevates 'entertainer' to 'Entertainer' – an effect, moreover, which is inappropriately communicable only to the eye that reads, not the ear that hears.

When the address became an essay, it came to open with an immediacy of common cause:

> I assume that we are all of one mind about the deplorable con-
> sequences of the schisms of Christianity, and are convinced of
> the vital importance of the reunion of Christendom.

But as originally uttered, the words 'I assume' had followed upon an attempted demonstration of what it is to be unassuming.

The occasion proved to be both like and unlike that at the Shakespeare Association, and not least in that humility was now demanded, and this is something very different from modesty's having been called for. 'Humility is the most difficult of all virtues to achieve' ('Shakespeare and the Stoicism of Seneca').

Some of Eliot's greatest apprehensions turn upon, turn to, humility. So in a poem he may quietly maintain that 'humility is endless', and this is a double truth: humility must never propose to itself an ulterior end, and humility must ever acknowledge the regression that lies in wait for it, for humility must not be proud of being humble, or proud of not being proud of being humble, or . . . 'Humility is endless': but Eliot, resisting the temptation of a proud apophthegm about humility, does not end section II of 'East Coker' there:

> The only wisdom we can hope to acquire
> Is the wisdom of humility: humility is endless.
>
> The houses are all gone under the sea.
>
> The dancers are all gone under the hill.[32]

To go back to the Anglo-Catholic Summer School of Sociology may be to judge that there the preambular remarks were flecked by

32 I draw here upon *T.S.Eliot and Prejudice* (1988), p.241.

the fact that on this occasion the humility did, in the nature of the case, propose to itself an ulterior end, was not 'endless'. Which might explain why the case is altered. It is true that here, too, as at the Shakespeare Association, the preamble does have its apt relation to the argument that follows, but now the aptness has started to feel collusive, as though what is uneasy in the preamble anticipates something uneasy in the body of the address. The denigration of those who, all-too-accustomed as they are to public speaking, 'descend to the rôle of a mere Entertainer' (the Bertrand Russells of this world, of *this* world), may be anticipating too comfortably the ensuing denigration of those who, unlike Eliot and his audience, are not Catholics.

> The non-Catholic, certainly the non-Christian philosopher, feeling no obligation to alter himself, and therefore no cogent need to understand himself, is apt to be under the sway of his prejudices, his social background, his individual tastes. So, I dare say, are we: but we at least, I hope, admit our duty to try to subdue them. This assertion may appear extremely presumptuous. But I speak not so much from my knowledge of economics, which is less than sketchy, as from my occasional acquaintance with economists.[33]

This lacks a due scepticism, not scepticism as opposed to religious conviction, but as opposed to the rhetorical coercions of 'certainly' and of 'therefore'. Is it really the case that there can be no cogent need to understand oneself for anyone who is not a Catholic? And that non-Catholics or non-Christians do not admit their duty to try to subdue their prejudices? The speaker does not seem on this occasion to be trying to subdue his own prejudices. And the concession as to being swayed by prejudices ('So, I dare say, are we') feels like a rhetorical concession only, in that 'I dare say' does not actually ask any daring on this particular occasion. Understanding yourself, alongside the presumptuous: this may call up not the Pope but Pope. 'Know then thyself, presume not God to scan'. The proper study of mankind is managing these matters with a greater respect for those who beg to differ. 'I hope' ('we at least, I hope, admit our

33 *Essays Ancient and Modern*, p.118.

duty to try to subdue them') may be long on hope and on faith but short on charity. As against the majority of Protestants,

> The Catholic with a more definite theology, and I hope a greater practice in self-examination, will make a more realistic observation of what he is doing and why.[34]

There are certain kinds of self-examination that this is not concerned to practise. A later self-examination by Eliot led to his examining these insistences more realistically, perhaps. There is a pertinent remark in the preface to *Essays Ancient and Modern* (which in 1936 was replacing *For Lancelot Andrewes*, 1928, which had gone out of print):

> I am aware that most of these papers date themselves, even when I have forgotten the dates. It may well be that in a few years' time I may wish to remove some from currency, as I have in the past.

'Catholicism and International Order' was later to be removed from currency, its currency having perhaps been seen to be in some respects debased. Humility is a more taxing aspiration than the very valuable thing modesty (it makes sense to speak of the modesty topos, but the humility topos is out of this world), and it is modesty that came to be emphasised in the preface to *Essays Ancient and Modern*:

> I observe that the advertisement of *For Lancelot Andrewes* advanced the claim that the essays 'had a unity of their own.' I do not know whether my ideals of unity are higher, or merely my pretensions more modest, than eight years ago; I offer this book, as the title implies, only as a miscellaneous collection, having no greater unity than that of having been written by the same person.
>
> T.S.E.

But what exactly does it imply by way of modesty, the play of the title *Essays Ancient and Modern*, given the ubiquitous indispensability of *Hymns Ancient and Modern*, a collection written by so many

---

34 *Essays Ancient and Modern*, p.137.

different people? And then, in conclusion, a nice unsoft touch, this initialling sequence:

> ...no greater unity than that of having been written by the same person.
>
> T.S.E.

☆ ☆ ☆

The public address is only one form that an occasion may take, but attending to it may have established some of the considerations which govern revision that is undertaken once the immediate occasion has passed, with the creator's thoughts now needing to be newly mediated. As always, there will be gains and losses: the gain of decorum when it comes to a new format or a new medium or a new occasion, alonside the loss of all that had been more than incidental to the original enterprise, the movement from the preamble to the ample body of the work itself.

In 1928, there was published a book that is called – if you were to judge by the spine – OF DRAMATICK POESIE *by* JOHN DRYDEN. To judge by the title-page, though:

[*See overleaf*]

*Of*
# DRAMATICK POESIE
## AN ESSAY
### 1668
*by* JOHN DRYDEN

*Preceded by a*
## DIALOGUE
### *on* POETIC DRAMA
### *by* T. S. ELIOT

*LONDON*
Frederick Etchells & Hugh Macdonald
1 9 2 8

Of this edition, 580 copies were for sale. Handsome, and once and for all, it was not intended to stay in print. And Eliot was right to judge that his dialogue was too good to be willingly let die – or to be let lie there only. So, four years later, *Selected Essays* includes the dialogue. Changed, though. 'A partial but significant shift' within the title ('une modification profonde', perhaps) settles upon 'A Dialogue on Dramatic Poetry', as against the original 'A Dialogue on Poetic Drama'. The larger change concerns the pairing of Dryden's essay with Eliot's, with Dryden courteously ushered in by Eliot. This change (from a book of about twenty pages of Eliot and seventy of Dryden) to a fifteen-page essay of Eliot's, standing alone: this change was inevitable, but (like many inevitable things) it is saddening, a real loss, albeit one that can be repaired by anyone who is an assiduous seeker after Dryden's truths as not only complimented but complemented by Eliot's truths. No less large is the further change that is regretfully (not regrettably, since it was the right thing to do) brought about when Eliot sacrifices his preface, which introduces not only his own essay but Dryden's too. Well known to Eliot scholars, it is less known to Eliot readers, and it merits quotation in full.[35] Once again, modesty rules. In its way.

### PREFACE

To compete with the late W.P.Ker and Mr. Nichol Smith and other scholars by attempting a learned introduction to Dryden's essay would be merely to commit a presumption and a super-fluity. The following method occurred to me as hitherto untried and as challenging no comparisons. Dryden composed his essay in the form of a dialogue, which might by some stretch of imagination have taken place between cultivated critics of his time. I have therefore composed a dialogue which may, with less stretch of imagination, for my language is less elegant and my periods shorter-breathed, be supposed to have taken place between half a dozen fairly intelligent men of our time. And as the topics discussed by Dryden's party were issues of his day, so are mine issues of our day. If I cannot add to the knowledge and

---

35 'Chaque version mérite d'être éditée ...'

understanding of Dryden, I can perhaps add to his glory by the contrast. But my purpose is, if possible, to throw the dialogue of Dryden into a rather new light, by the great contrast between the topics, and between the attitudes towards them. For this the centuries are responsible. My dialogue represents the scraps of many actual conversations at divers times and in divers circumstances; and is intended to collect some representative topics among those which arise in any such conversation to-day. Dryden and his friends could discuss a "dramatic poetry" which actually existed, which was still being written; and their aim was therefore to construct its critical laws. We, on the other hand, are always discussing something which does not exist but which we should like to have brought into existence; so we are not occupied with critical laws; and so we range over a wide field of speculation, asking many questions and answering none.

The dialogue is a form even more convenient for my purpose than it was for Dryden's. Dryden had written great plays; but the contemporary critic has not written a great play, so is in a weak position for laying down the law about plays. If he dogmatised, he would expose himself to the adjuration to go and write the poetic drama of the future instead of talking about it. But the dialogue form enables me to discuss the subject without pretending to come to any conclusion. Furthermore, Dryden's own opinions issue quite clearly from his dialogue; I have no clear opinions on this subject. Hence I have distributed my own theories quite indiscriminately among the speakers; and the reader must not try to identify the persons in the dialogue with myself or anyone else. They are not even fictions; they are merely voices; a half-dozen men who may be imagined as sitting in a tavern after lunch, lingering over port and conversation at an hour when they should all be doing something else.

T. S. ELIOT

The disclaimers are manifold: 'without pretending to', 'quite indiscriminately', 'not even fictions', 'when they should all be doing something else' – as though he, the author, should perhaps have been doing something else . . .

Such is the ending, but from the start the provocations have been estimable. The first two words announce it all, though they do not say it all: *To compete*. . . To compete with W. P. Ker or with David Nichol Smith? Of course not, this would be 'merely to commit a presumption and a superfluity'.[36] But the real challenge is how not to enter into competition, not with Dryden scholars, but with Dryden. It is therefore with something of a flat-tongued challenge in itself that Eliot moves from Ker and Nichol Smith to the courteous effrontery of this: 'The following method occurred to me as hitherto untried and as challenging no comparisons'. No comparison with the scholars, understood, but the understanding then is alive to its own tacit comedy.[37] If there were ever an enterprise that announced itself as challenging comparisons, it would have to be this:

*Of*
DRAMATICK POESIE
AN ESSAY
1668
*by* JOHN DRYDEN


*Preceded by a*
DIALOGUE
*on* POETIC DRAMA
*by* T. S. ELIOT


Not that Eliot then has his work cut out in establishing the essential modesties, for what is at play is play, not work. His caveats are fair warning. That his dialogue has less stretch of imagination, that his language is less elegant and his periods shorter-breathed: these are not admissions but acknowledgments, and they cost their speaker neither too little nor too much, leading as they do to the poised scruple of an *If* . . . (not the cadging solicitation of a *Given that* . . .): 'If I cannot add to the knowledge and understanding of Dryden, I

36 Again *merely* has its role to play on these occasions, as with 'or merely my pretensions more modest', 'mere journalist', and 'mere Entertainer'.
37 Of Eliot scholar-critics, William Arrowsmith is the one who most imaginatively followed Eliot's choice of the dialogue-form. See his 'Eros in Terre Haute: T.S.Eliot's "Lune de Miel"', *The New Criterion* (October 1982).

can perhaps add to his glory by the contrast'. The knowledge and understanding *of* Dryden are at once that which others have brought to him and Dryden's own.

The entire continuity of the preface with what follows – Eliot's dialogue and Dryden's essay – is explicit and unmistakable. This is not to say that the subsequent dropping of the preface renders the dialogue deficient, but it does remind us that such sacrifices (we protect ourselves against the pain of sacrifice by adopting the term *cost-benefit*) must be not just accepted but embraced. Much was lost when 'A Dialogue on Dramatic Poetry' gained its place in *Selected Essays*. Not only Eliot's relaxed intelligence (not a relaxing of his intelligence) as to the enterprise itself, but a sense of how much was already, back in 1928, fecundating his ambitions in drama. He makes the creative point as to criticism:

> Dryden had written great plays; but the contemporary critic has not written a great play, so is in a weak position for laying down the law about plays. If he dogmatised, he would expose himself to the adjuration to go and write the poetic drama of the future instead of talking about it.

In the immediate future, Eliot was to go and write. *Sweeney Agonistes: Fragments of an Aristophanic Melodrama* was to issue four years later, and *The Rock*, two years after that, with *Murder in the Cathedral* in 1935. His phrasing in 1928 had been marked by a felicitous syntactical equivocation: 'We, on the other hand, are always discussing something which does not exist but which we should like to have brought into existence'. Is it that we should like a poetic drama to have been brought into existence, or that we should like to be the ones to have done so? *Which we should like to have brought into existence.*

'A Dialogue on Dramatic Poetry' lost not only its preface but its pairing and its sharing an occasion with John Dryden. Similar adjustments and losses are necessarily involved when a series exists. Each individual Ariel poem of Eliot's (with some sense, moreover, of the series as it extended beyond Eliot) is changed by its being at once autonomous and part of a larger union and communion; hence Eliot's preservation of the category, 'Ariel Poems', for the five poems that date from 1927, 1928, 1929, 1930 and – cultivated anew

– 'The Cultivation of Christmas Trees' in 1954. Within the prose, the central instance is Eliot's contribution to the series 'The Poets on the Poets', his seventy-page book, *Dante*. It was the second volume in the series. Geoffrey Hill thinks ill of the series, or more exactly judges that it colluded with some regrettably propitiatory tendencies in Eliot's criticism:[38]

> The Faber monographs were designed as antepasts to enjoyment and the refining of taste. There are values and virtues more significant than enjoyment, which shares with other taste-derived qualities an air of condescension, of the proprietorial. Enjoyment of this kind is closely related to apathy. Eliot's *Dante*, preceded in the series by V. Sackville-West's *Marvell*, was itself followed by Lascelles Abercrombie's *Wordsworth*, Humbert Wolfe's *Tennyson* and Edmund Blunden's *Coleridge*.[39]

Or, gilt by association.

Eliot has often been judged guilty of association with the politics of Charles Maurras, right-wing, to say nothing of French, and this charge raises a question about revision and about whether things can ever be revised away. Geoffrey Hill has deplored the dedicatory page of Eliot's *Dante* in 1929, with its epigraph:

> As an instance of Eliot's aestheticized – and aestheticizing – politics, consider the epigraph to his *Dante*, a sentence taken from *Le Conseil de Dante*, a (then) recently published book by Charles Maurras, the founder of *Action Française* to whom Eliot's monograph is dedicated: 'La sensibilité, sauvée d'elle-même et conduite

38 Hill has his own sombrely comical deployment of the modesty topos in opening his essay on Dante, 'Between Politics and Eternity': 'The editorial brief for contributions to *The Poets' Dante* invites a response to several questions which presuppose – if I understand them – some degree of significant prior involvement with Dante's life and writings: significant to the contributor, that is. While not wishing to tap into the confessional mode, I have to say that my own (insignificant) involvement with Dante began no earlier than mid-summer 1999 when I belatedly agreed to write a piece for this collection. If for nothing else, I decided, the necessary labor would serve as a challenge to my own ignorance'. (*The Poets' Dante*, ed. Peter S. Hawkins and Rachel Jacoff, 2001, p.319.) A confession or profession of ignorance is *de rigueur* on these occasions.

39 *The Poets' Dante*, pp.320–1.

dans l'ordre, est devenue un principe de perfection' (Sensibility, redeemed from itself and reduced to order, became a basis of perfection). These words assist our understanding of Eliot's *Ash-Wednesday*, but they do nothing to strengthen our grasp of the *Comedy*.[40]

But when Eliot reprinted his *Dante*, in the only form in which he kept it in print, as section IV of his *Selected Essays*, he dropped the dedication and the epigraph. This is not to say that he thereby disclaimed (or, slightly different, could disclaim) the original commitment, but it might be judged to entail some modification of the charge against him, that in aestheticizing politics he does nothing to strengthen our grasp of Dante. (A charge that is in any case left as say-so, and so does nothing to strengthen our grasp of exactly what is at issue.) Hill himself originally introduced *Mercian Hymns* in 1971 with a sixteen-line prose epigraph on the conduct of government, from an English right-wing Charles, Charles Sisson. Is this, too, an instance of a poet's aestheticized and aestheticizing politics? It did nothing to strengthen our grasp of *Mercian Hymns* – or so presumably Hill judged when he decided to drop it. And when the epigraph disappeared from *Mercian Hymns*, did nothing about the poet's responsibility for the epigraph change?

But the large-scale revision of Eliot's *Dante* is elsewhere, in the decision that, once this was no longer a book on its own while part of a series, but rather a section within a book of essays, the original preface had to go. Here too there had been an occasion, and a sense of occasion. And here too we have a distinctive work of criticism by Eliot that is perfectly well known to Eliot scholars but not to most readers of Eliot.

## PREFACE

If my task had been to produce another brief 'introduction to the study of Dante' I should have been incompetent to perform it. But in a series of essays of 'Poets on Poets' the undertaking, as I understand it, is quite a different one. A contemporary writer of verse, in writing a pamphlet of this description, is required

40 *The Poets' Dante*, p.329.

only to give a faithful account of his acquaintance with the poet of whom he writes. This, and no more, I can do; and this is the only way in which I can treat an author of whom so much has been written, that can make any pretence to novelty. I have found no other poet than Dante to whom I could apply continually, for many purposes, and with much profit, during a familiarity of twenty years. I am not a Dante scholar; my Italian is chiefly self-taught, and learnt primarily in order to read Dante; I need still to make constant reference to translations. Yet it has occurred to me that by relating the process of my own gradual and still very imperfect knowledge of Dante, I might give some help to persons who must begin where I began – with a public school knowledge of Latin, a traveller's smattering of Italian, and a literal translation beside the text. For this reason my order, in the following chapters, is the order of my own initiation. I begin with detail, and approach the general scheme. I began myself with passages of the *Inferno* which I could understand, passed on to the *Purgatorio* in the same way, and only after years of experience began to appreciate the *Paradiso*; from which I reverted to the other parts of the poem and slowly realized the unity of the whole. I believe that it is quite natural and right to tackle the *Vita Nuova* afterwards. For an English reader who reads the *Vita Nuova* too soon is in danger of reading it under Pre-Raphaelite influence.

My purpose has been to persuade the reader first of the importance of Dante as a master – I may even say, *the* master – for a poet writing to-day in any language. And there ensues from that, the importance of Dante to anyone who would appreciate modern poetry, in any language. I should not trust the opinion of anyone who pretended to judge modern verse without knowing Homer, Dante, and Shakespeare. It does not in the least follow that a *poet* is negligible because he does not know these three.

Having thus excused this book, I do not feel called upon to give any bibliography. Anyone can easily discover more Dante bibliography than anyone can use. But I should like to mention one book which has been of use to me: the *Dante* of Professor Charles Grandgent of Harvard. I owe something to an essay by Mr. Ezra Pound in his *Spirit of Romance*, but more to his table-talk; and I owe something to Mr. Santayana's essay in *Three Philosophical Poets*. And one should at least glance at the *Readings* of

W.W.Vernon in order to see how far into mediaeval philosophy, theology, science, and literature a thorough study of Dante must go.

The reader whom I have kept in mind, in writing this essay, is the reader who commences his reading of Dante with Messrs. Dent's invaluable *Temple Classics* edition (3 volumes at 2*s.* each). For this reason I have in quotations followed the *Temple Classics* edition text, and have followed pretty closely the translation in the same volumes. It is hardly necessary to say that where my version varies it nowhere pretends to greater accuracy than that excellent translation. Anyone who reads my essay before attempting Dante at all will be likely to turn next to the *Temple Classics* edition, with its text and translation on opposite pages. There is something to be said for Longfellow's, and something for Norton's translation; but for anyone who can follow the Italian even gropingly the Temple translation is the best.

Here again is the immediate limitation upon what competence is claimed; the studied diminution of standing (Eliot as 'a contemporary writer of verse', with this hardback book as 'a pamphlet'); the minimizing of the enterprise ('required only to give a faithful account of his acquaintance with the poet of whom he writes'); the abjuration of 'any pretence to . . .'; and the disclaiming of scholarly authority ('I am not a Dante scholar', 'I need still to make constant reference to translations', 'my own gradual and still very imperfect knowledge of Dante').[41] These are honest admissions, and they ring the more true because of the quiet comedy that plays over them, as in the happiness that sets 'invaluable' against 'at 2*s.* each'. 'Having thus excused this book . . .'? Excuse me.

The preface went. But, once again, something invaluable (more than two shillings' worth) went at the same time. For the admissions had amounted to a substantiated clarification. 'This, and no more, I can do'. Is not a reader of Eliot's Dante, whether as a book in a series or as a series of three essays, helped by being told all this?

41 I learn from Ronald Schuchard that Eliot wrote to Pound on 9 December 1929 that the Dante book "is merely a small *auto*biographical fragment, not a contribution to scholarship for my Ph.D." (*Eliot's Dark Angel*, 1999, p.252.) Yet the autobiographical element was that which was most reduced when the book became a section of *Selected Essays*.

There is the form of words, *It is hardly necessary to say* . . . : these things had once needed to be said, why was it now no longer necessary to say them? They have to be done without. 'This, and no more, I can do'. This, and no less, he had done. And not the least of the rewards that had come with *Dante* in its original form, autobiographically prefaced, had been its personal transparency, its forthcomingness, and its reminder as to how and why an educative decision may be made. 'My Italian is chiefly self-taught, *and learnt primarily in order to read Dante*': my emphasis, but also tacitly Eliot's, in its telling reminder of what may be the better way round. (It is not that he is able to read Dante because he has some Italian, but that he has some Italian because he yearns to read Dante.)

When the preface went, other reflections went too. As it came to be represented in *Selected Essays*,[42] the commentary runs at one point like this:

> The language of each great English poet is his own language; the language of Dante is the perfection of a common language. In a sense, it is more pedestrian than that of Dryden or Pope. If you follow Dante without talent, you will at worst be pedestrian and flat; if you follow Shakespeare or Pope without talent, you will make an utter fool of yourself.
> But if one has learnt this much from the *Inferno*...

But as originally published, there had been an intervening paragraph, one that is imaginatively continuous with the preface and its self-examination:

> Nevertheless, the *simple* style of which Dante is the greatest master is a very difficult style. In twenty years I have written about a dozen lines in that style successfully; and compared to the dullest passage of the *Divine Comedy*, they are 'as straw'. So I believe that it is difficult.[43]

This is phrasing that is to be believed, audibly authenticated in the movement from 'a very difficult style' to 'So I believe that it is

---

42 *Selected Essays*, p.252.
43 *Dante*, pp.35–36. Eliot alludes to Job 41:27, 'He esteemeth iron as straw, and brass as rotten wood'.

difficult'. Had any such claim, even to so limited a success, come to seem inordinate to Eliot? Had he wearied of being asked questions as to which were the dozen lines, exactly? Had he become unwilling, by 1932, to make it sound as though he were tempted to give up the struggle? Hearteningly, his two greatest achievements as to Dante were still to come: the Dantesque section of 'Little Gidding' (1942), 'In the uncertain hour before the morning...', and the talk to the Italian Institute in 1950, 'What Dante Means to Me', deep and deeply moving.

*Dante* (1929) has raised the question of epigraphs, a vast and subtle subject in itself, and a resource where Eliot the poet undertook some particularly revelatory revisions.[44] Let me do no more than point briefly to Eliot's decision and revision in a case within the prose. The essay 'Christopher Marlowe', in the form in which it is most frequently met (within *Selected Essays*), begins with equanimity:

> Swinburne observes of Marlowe that 'the father of English tragedy and the creator of English blank verse was therefore also the teacher and the guide of Shakespeare'.

Fair enough. But as originally published in 1919, and as kept alive in *The Sacred Wood* (1920, and continuing alongside *Selected Essays* from 1932), this same essay – under a different title, 'Notes on the Blank Verse of Christopher Marlowe'[45] – had chosen to pounce:

> 'Marloe was stabd with a dagger, and dyed swearing'

> A more friendly critic, Mr A.C. Swinburne, observes of Marlowe that 'the father of English tragedy and the creator of English blank verse was therefore also the teacher and the guide of Shakespeare'.

44 The subject of a critically informative Cambridge doctoral thesis (2003) by Jennifer Formichelli.
45 Originally, in *Art & Letters* (Autumn 1919), 'Some Notes on the Blank Verse of Christopher Marlowe'. *Notes towards the Definition of Culture* (1948) had employed a different article when in 1943 it had been a series of articles: 'Notes towards a Definition of Culture'.

This is much more penetrating as an opening, with its intimation as to one form that practical criticism might legitimately take, the sudden death itself an instance of that savage farce which the essay goes on to see as characteristic of Marlowe's work. 'A more friendly critic': yes, I suppose you could say that. Even the decorum of '*Mr A. C. Swinburne*' maintains the preposterous propriety, while the fate of the father of tragedy, the teacher of Shakespeare, turns out to be the parricide that awaits fathers and teachers. How vividly the original opening had bloomed. The later propriety is a shade proper. You miss the chaffing impudence, which then has its darker underside of 'savage comic humour', such as 'attains its effects by something not unlike caricature', in the conclusive words of the essay.

But let me conclude this opening discussion of Eliot's decisions and revisions within openings, by turning to one more form, a simple form, that an occasion may take: the occasion of a review. Eliot's review of Arthur Symons, *Baudelaire: Prose and Poetry*, was published in *The Dial* (May 1927). It was reprinted as 'Baudelaire in Our Time' in *For Lancelot Andrewes* (1927), and likewise in the collection that replaced this, *Essays Ancient and Modern* (1936). Eliot had by this later date come to feel uneasy about '. . . in our Time': '"our time" is perhaps over'.[46] What was over and done with after only six months had passed (from May 1927 to November 1927) was the paragraph that had originally opened the review-essay, a paragraph for which the occasion had passed. In its deploring immodesty of several kinds, it stands as a reminder of the need for, as well as the difficulty of, modesty. Eliot, who had for two years been exercising responsibility within a publishing house, was moved to deplore a publisher's malpractice, and his protest (which was lost in the reprinting) has lost none of its force and none of its applicability to 'our time':

> First I must protest against the words *Baudelaire Complete* which the publishers have placed on the wrapper of this book. There are two hundred and seventy-eight pages of translation. Mr Symons has translated most, but not all, of Les Fleurs du Mal: he has not included the section Spleen et Idéal, and even the most

46 Preface to *Essays Ancient and Modern*.

casual admirer of Baudelaire will miss Le Voyage; he has translated part, but by no means all, of Les Paradis Artificiels; only the Petits Poèmes en Prose are complete. But even if Mr Symons had given us the whole of the poetry, and the whole of the Paradis Artificiels, the word *Complete* would still be deplorable. There are now two fine editions of Baudelaire Complete in process of publication: that of Conard and that of La Nouvelle Revue Française; each runs to about fifteen volumes. In the case of many authors, this misstatement would not have so much mattered; for even some voluminous authors can be judged fairly by a very small part of their work. But not Baudelaire. It is now becoming understood that Baudelaire is one of the few poets who wrote nothing, either prose or verse, that is negligible. To understand Baudelaire you must read the whole of Baudelaire. And nothing that he wrote is without importance. He was a great poet; he was a great critic. And he was also a man with a profound attitude toward life, for the study of which we need every scrap of his writing. To call this volume "Baudelaire Complete" is to mislead the public.

It would have been an uncharacteristic and crude immodesty for Eliot in 1927 to have had himself in mind at all there. But we are not prevented from having him in mind.[47]

For it is now becoming understood that Eliot is one of the few poets who wrote nothing, either prose or verse, that is negligible. To understand Eliot you must read the whole of Eliot. And nothing that he wrote is without importance. He was a great poet; he was a great critic. And he was also a man with a profound attitude toward life, for the study of which we need every scrap of his writing.

Which includes the scraps, and the more than scraps, that he came to scrap. Which includes that very paragraph.

47 As has Ronald Schuchard, in his fascinatingly detailed 'Appendix: American Publishers and the Transmission of T.S.Eliot's Prose', in *Eliot's Dark Angel* (1999).

# In the Middle

To move from Eliot's revision, after publication, of how he had begun a piece (an address or an essay or a review), to how he proceeded within a piece: this is not to move away from the continuing centrality of all such revision's relation to self-criticism, to a due modesty and to a proper pride. So let me start upon these middle matters by reverting to a case I gave of Eliot's dropping the opening paragraph of an address, that of 'Shakespeare and the Stoicism of Seneca'.

Within the large-scale critical feat that mounts to the challenging exposé of 'the last great speech of Othello', there is a small-scale critical feat, one that amounts to a great deal but is incarnate in something that is no more than tiny: the crucial post-publication revision by which parentheses (round brackets, lunulae)[1] were added to encompass a remarkable aside.[2]

---

1 (I learnt of lunulae, little moons, a term that we owe to Erasmus, from John Lennard's imaginative and learnèd study of the higher punctuation, *But I Digress*, 1991.)

2 On Eliot's artistry with parentheses, see the present author's *The Force of Poetry* (1984), pp. 307–9, contemplating such accomplishments as these:

(Why should the agèd eagle stretch its wings?)
*(Ash-Wednesday)*

(Another hid his eyes behind his wing)
*(The Waste Land)*

Parentheses, especially when it is by lunulae that they are sig-
nalled – as not all parenthetical remarks are, this one for instance
not being so, being dashed off – are themselves the matter of a middle. They have something in the middle of them, and they would
constitute a very strange opening, and a strange closing, this last
effect being behind Eliot's fun and games within 'Five-Finger
Exercises'. He chose to end 'Lines to Ralph Hodgson Esqre', which
had begun 'How delightful to meet Mr. Hodgson!', with a circling
back and then an encircled line:

> How delightful to meet Mr. Hodgson!
> (Everyone wants to meet *him*).

This last line is one of four parenthesized lines in the poem, with one
of them enacting its apartness of meaning before our very regard:

> Who is worshipped by all waitresses
> (They regard him as something apart)
> While on his palate fine he presses
> The juice of the gooseberry tart.

The next poem in the sequence of 'Five-Finger Exercises', which had
contrastingly begun 'How unpleasant to meet Mr. Eliot!' (contrasting
with the poem for Hodgson as well as with Edward Lear's original
comic immodesty, 'How pleasant to know Mr Lear!', allusion being
a further form that revision may take), was likewise to conclude
with such encirclings but with the sole such parenthesized line in
the poem:

And, most powerfully (this, a *pre*-publication revision of 'The Death of St.
Narcissus'):

> Only
> There is shadow under this red rock,
> (Come in under the shadow of this red rock),
> And I will show you something different from either
> Your shadow at morning striding behind you
> Or your shadow at evening rising to meet you;
> I will show you fear in a handful of dust.
> (*The Waste Land*)

> How unpleasant to meet Mr. Eliot!
> (Whether his mouth be open or shut).

Comedy, open and shut, finds itself tucked up within parentheses. Such comedy is seriously deployed within Eliot's criticism, as when – explaining what his two pieces on Milton had been up to – Eliot ends his hundred-word parenthesis, that had begun *(But when I wrote my first essay on Milton…*, with this handsome gratuity: … *This reference to Milton is parenthetical.)*[3]

Such is comedy. By contrast, tragedy might enter into lunulae that suggest mortal moons, enduring the eclipse of hope. As when Eliot added, in post-publication revision of his thoughts on Othello, the harbouring marks of punctuation here:

> I have always felt that I have never read a more terrible exposure of human weakness – of universal human weakness – than the last great speech of Othello. (I am ignorant whether anyone else has ever adopted this view, and it may appear subjective and fantastic in the extreme.)[4]

'I am ignorant whether …': this invokes the necessary modesty that had come to ask to be characterized by parentheses, with their particular power to suggest that they contain at once a crux and an aside.[5]

The acumen of Eliot's commentary is fostered by its being continuous with the very words of the play. In the speech that Eliot immediately quotes, we hear Othello's cry, 'Perplex'd in the extreme'. (Eliot's 'fantastic in the extreme'.) Earlier in the scene, we have heard Emilia's cry against Othello, 'As ignorant as dirt'. (Eliot's 'I am ignorant' – a phrasing which, in the original address, had itself been a development of the stylized modesty that had initially announced the need to 'conceal my ignorance'.) Earlier in the play

---

3 My italics, to clarify. *To Criticize the Critic* (1965), pp. 23–24.
4 *Selected Essays*, p.130. No lunulae in the printed lecture.
5 As in the central moment of Geoffrey Hill's profound evocation of the death-camps, 'September Song', which has this at its heart:
> (I have made
> an elegy for myself it
> is true)

(II i), there had been Iago's cry against the pair of them, Othello and Desdemona: 'Mark with what violence she first loved the Moor, but for bragging and telling her fantastical lies'. (Eliot's 'fantastic in the extreme'.) Othello is dishonoured for bragging and telling fantastical lies. Eliot may be honoured for not bragging and for telling truths, truths about Othello's lying to himself, or rather about his all-too-human self-deception. Eliot himself confesses ignorance but professes truth, this turn itself being implicated in a post-publication revision that Eliot was to make when reconsidering his praise of F. H. Bradley's 'habit of discomfiting an opponent with a sudden confession' – no, 'a sudden profession of ignorance'.[6]

But then all of Eliot's praise of Bradley at this point is germane to Eliot himself and to the present enterprise:

> And many readers, having in mind Bradley's polemical irony and his obvious zest in using it, his habit of discomfiting an opponent with a sudden profession of ignorance, of inability to understand, or of incapacity for abstruse thought,[7] have concluded that this is all a mere pose – and even a somewhat unscrupulous one. But deeper study of Bradley's mind convinces us that the modesty is real, and his irony the weapon of a modest and highly sensitive man.

Very humane, the movement from 'having in mind Bradley's . . .' to 'Bradley's mind'. Such a mind was Eliot's.

Eliot's criticism belongs to the rare kind that rises to creativity, in rising to another's creativity thereby rising to its own. The distinction between criticism and creation is itself given salience within Eliot's revisions. There is 'The Function of Criticism': 'No exponent of criticism (in this limited sense) has, I presume, ever made the preposterous assumption that criticism is an autonomous activity' (*The Criterion*, October 1923). In *Selected Essays*, 'autonomous' was changed to 'autotelic'.[8] And there is 'Whether Rostand Had Something about Him', which became, in its extensive revision for

---

6 *Times Literary Supplement* (29 December 1927); revised *Selected Essays*, pp.444–5.
7 Eliot (*New English Weekly*, 16 May 1946): 'for I have no gift whatever for abstruse thinking'.
8 *Selected Essays*, p.24.

*The Sacred Wood*, ' "Rhetoric" and Poetic Drama'. Here, there was lost a profound aside that is itself at once definition, creation and criticism:

> Instead of seeking, therefore, a definition (definition is a labour of creation rather than of criticism), we might do better to find a 'rhetorical' period of a rhetoric similar to Rostand's. . .[9]

How deftly the passing parenthesis encompasses so much. When it was among the commentary that was subsequently displaced, Eliot's self-criticism in revision showed itself, for once, misplaced. The contrast might be with a moment, when again discussing this same nexus (the relation of criticism to creation), Eliot was wisely moved to cut, after publication, a passing remark that similarly had within itself the passing punctuation that is parenthesis. As originally published in *The Criterion* (October 1923), the paragraph of 'The Function of Criticism' had begun like this:

> But no writer is completely self-sufficient, and many creative writers have a critical activity which is not all discharged into their work. Some seem to require to keep their critical powers in condition for the real work by exercising them miscellaneously; others, on completing a work, need to continue the critical activity by commenting on it. *Coleridge (if you like it) had to write about others; Dryden had to write about his own preoccupations. I do not suppose Mr Joyce has to do either.* There is no general rule.[10]

The instances that I have italicized had to go, presumably as too tendentiously offhand. Their comedy had its charm (if you like it),[11] but the draw was too close to the drawl, and too much invited the

9 *Athenaeum* (25 July 1919).
10 *The Criterion*, ii (October 1923) 39. Revised *Selected Essays*, p.31.
11 Elsewhere, Eliot ceased to like the phrase *(if you like)*; he dropped it, in post-publication revision, from 'Christopher Marlowe': 'Shakespeare is "universal" (if you like) because he has more of these tones than anyone else'. (Still so in *The Sacred Wood*, 1920, p.79, but dropped from *Selected Essays*, p.119. Please note that I have not made it my business, though it would be the business of a thorough edition of Eliot's prose, to record at what moment, for what publication, Eliot made a particular revision. For economy's sake, I move in my documentation from the original texts to the final versions, which are mostly those to be found

riposte, 'and you, sir?'. (I do not suppose Mr Eliot has to do either.) Best to move immediately to 'There is no general rule'.

The revision of criticism remains different from the revision of art, for instance the art of poetry – not because art does not suppose that it must remain faithful to something that is not of its making, something that had been and is there, but because criticism's fidelity to *another's* enterprise is of a different nature and may entail different responsibilities. For instance, art may claim, with all truth, that its showing things as they are *not* is to the point, as in surrealism and romance; whereas the claim can, in criticism, operate only within narrow limits – the narrow limits of acknowledged hyperbole, for instance.

If I had to choose a single instance of Eliot's genius in revising his critical prose, it would be the essay on Ben Jonson, which was published anonymously in the *Times Literary Supplement* (13 November 1919) and then collected, the next year, in *The Sacred Wood*. The achievement in this immediate revision, the full releasing of so much that had in some places only lurked, is to me on the scale of D. H. Lawrence's famous and amazing re-imagining of the conclusion to his haunting story, 'Odour of Chrysanthemums'.

in *Selected Essays* though there are the cases of essays that were reprinted but not then collected in *Selected Essays*.)

Eliot often cut out disparagements that he had come to think cheap. Of Matthew Arnold: 'Certainly he gives me the impression *(and his operation is largely the giving of impressions)* that Culture (as he uses the term) is something more comprehensive than religion'. The words that I have italicized, which figured in 'Cultural Forces in the Human Order' (*Prospect for Christendom*, ed. Maurice B. Reckitt, 1945, p.62), were dropped from *Notes towards the Definition of Culture* (1948), p.28. So was a factitious hesitation: 'The effect of thinness – *I hesitate to say superficiality* – which Arnold's abstract culture makes upon a modern reader' (*Prospect for Christendom*, p.58; revised in *Notes towards the Definition of Culture*, p.22). These are importantly honourable acts of self-criticism, in their reconsidering the criticisms passed upon others. Sometimes it took a while for Eliot to come to forgive those who had, he judged, ill-judged him. The slighting reference in 'The Frontiers of Criticism' (1956) to 'a Mr. Bateson' was replaced, first, by the inadvertent comedy of 'Mr. F.E. Bateson' (the slightly wrong initials being under the influence, I suspect, of F.E.Smith – 'Chuck it, Bateson'?), but in the end by the simple truth, 'Mr. F.W. Bateson'. (*On Poetry and Poets*, 1957, p. 111, corrected in later impressions.)

Ask yourself what you would make of Eliot's great critical essay[12] if it were to lack, for instance, as it had originally done, the substantial paragraph begining 'Jonson is the legitimate heir of Marlowe', with its exemplary quoting, or the subsequent three pages (likewise added in 1920) that so persuasively delineate the art of Jonson, 'an art of caricature, of great caricature, like Marlowe's'.[13]

There is an indubitability about such revisions that is greatly to Eliot's credit. But at this point something of an excursus is called for, in that there are dubitabilities which may have to be judged to be to the publisher's, or the several publishers', discredit. Dubitabilities: that is, discrepancies between the received Eliot text and the original that may well be, not revisions, but errors. One of the glum rewards of collating (in quest of revisions) the different versions that reached publication has turned out to be the identification of some moments that are certainly puzzling and that are probably carelessnesses somewhere in the publishing process. If I give some of these here, it is partly to indicate that there is always likely to be a gray area of uncertainty, and partly to fortify the case for a fully scrupulous edition of Eliot's writings.

To start with a few points of detail. 'A Dialogue on Dramatic Poetry' made sense in 1928 when it said of Shaw, Pinero and Coward that 'Their cleverness lies in finding out how their audiences

12  The importance of which to Eliot's own creativity as a poet has been demonstrated by William H. Pritchard, 'Reading *The Waste Land* Today', *Essays in Criticism* (April 1969).
13  *Selected Essays*, p.154, and pp.156–159, from 'A writer of power and intelligence . . .', to 'He did not get the third dimension, but he was not trying to get it'. To these inspired additions there must be added the further credit of circumspect deletion when the essay moved from *The Sacred Wood* to *Selected Essays*. The six words at the end of the following sentence were despatched in revision: 'And to see him as a contemporary does not so much require the power of putting ourselves into seventeenth-century London as it requires the power of setting Jonson in our London; a more difficult triumph of divination'. Too triumphant a tone, as though not just good at divination but divinely inspired. (*The Sacred Wood*, p.106; revised as *Selected Essays*, p.148.) There likewise vanished, in the same move, a moment of large intellectuality that Eliot must have come to feel had an element of arcane bluff about it: 'It is a world like Lobatchevsky's; the worlds created by Jonson are like systems of non-Euclidean geometry'. (*The Sacred Wood*, pp.116–7; revised as *Selected Essays*, p.156.)

would like to behave, and encouraging them to do it by exhibiting personages behaving in that way'.[14] As given in *Selected Essays*, the remark no longer really makes sense: 'Their cleverness lies in finding out how much their audiences would like to behave, and encouraging them to do it by exhibiting personages behaving in that way'.[15] How much? Contrast this, which looks clearly a mistake (to me, at least), with a different dubiety, the change from the 1928 reading in this same dialogue, 'Human nature does not change. Another double port, please', to '. . . Another port, please'.[16] How much of a muchness is this? Did Eliot decide that a double port was a bit much, especially 'in a tavern after lunch'? Human nature does not change, but it may be that Eliot did. There is perhaps no knowing.

Such examples may seem so small as to be frivolous, though nothing about a great writer's wording is ever so small as not to be *possibly* of moment. The larger, potentially more mischievous, instances come when what we have been given to read of late does make a modicum of sense, or a simulacrum of it, but nevertheless makes less sense than what used to be there.

For example, as originally published, anonymously, in the *Times Literary Supplement* (27 May 1920), Eliot's words in 'Philip Massinger' were these: 'We must employ Mr. Cruickshank's method to examine Mr. Cruickshank's judgments; and perhaps the most important judgment to which he has committed himself is this'. In *Selected Essays*, this has read, since 1932: 'We must employ Mr. Cruickshank's judgments; and perhaps the most important judgment to which he has committed himself is this'.[17] But employing Mr. Cruickshank's judgments, as against employing his method, looks askew. Is the discrepancy not a simple error, one that came about because someone's eye moved inadvertently from the first occurrence of the words *Mr. Cruickshank's* to their second occurrence three words later? Should not the text of the essay in *Selected Essays* be brought into line here with the original?

14 *Of Dramatick Poesie . . . Preceded by a Dialogue on Poetic Drama by T.S.Eliot* (1928), p.xiii.
15 *Selected Essays*, p.45.
16 (1928), p.xviii. *Selected Essays*, p.50.
17 *Selected Essays*, p.206.

The simple scribal error[18] may lurk behind a similar moment in the first Milton essay. Within its original form, 'A Note on the Verse of John Milton' (1936), one asseveration ran:

> This kind of 'rhetoric' is not necessarily bad in itself, though likely to be bad in its influence; and it may be considered bad in relation to the historical life of a language as a whole.

But as it runs within 'Milton I',[19] this cuts a corner:

> This kind of "rhetoric" is not necessarily bad in its influence; but it may be considered bad in relation to the historical life of a language as a whole.

A different thing to say, and harder to follow. Is this not the same commonplace error, the eye mistakenly taking up not the first 'bad' but the second one half-a-dozen words later? And should not this, too, be emended?

Unfortunately, most of us most of the time read with something less than entire attention. How else could it be that for so long the second Milton essay of Eliot's should have perpetrated, without (apparently) remark from its readers, the following sequence, or rather non-sequence, of thought?

> Of some great poetry one has difficulty in pronouncing just what it is, what infinitesimal touch, that has made all the difference from a plain statement which anyone could make; the slight transformation which, while it leaves a plain statement a plain statement, has always the maximal, never the minimal, alteration of ordinary language.

Three times this speaks (decorously) of 'a plain statement', while not – or rather, while no longer – issuing in a plain statement itself. 'The slight transformation which, while it leaves a plain statement

---

18 Compare haplography, 'the unintentional writing of a letter or word, or series of letters or words, once, when it should be written twice'. The opposite of dittography, 'the unintentional repetition of a letter or word, or series of letters or words, by a copyist'.

19 In *On Poetry and Poets*, British and American editions, and in *Milton: Two Studies*.

a plain statement, has always the maximal, never the minimal, alteration of ordinary language'? I beg your pardon? But the statement in the original had been perfectly plain, moving on, by way of contrast, from one kind of great poetry to Milton's kind:

> ... the slight transformation which, while it leaves a plain statement a plain statement, has *made it at the same time great poetry. In Milton there is* always the maximal, never the minimal, alteration of ordinary language.[20]

The disappearance of the words italicized comes (if I am right) to something more and something less than a 'slight transformation'.

It is not only the literary criticism that has so suffered, but the religious writing, too. In the only form in which it has long been available, that within *Selected Essays*, 'The *Pensées* of Pascal' is apparently committed to a train of thought that arrives at no sense literal or spiritual.

> A moment of Jansenism may naturally take place, and take place rightly, in the individual; particularly in the life of a man of great and intense intellectual powers, who cannot avoid seeing through human beings and observing the vanity of their thoughts and of their avocations, their dishonesty and self-deception, the insincerity of their emotions, their cowardice, the pettiness of their real ambitions. Actually, considering that much greater maturity is required for these qualities, than for any mathematical or scientific greatness, how easily his brooding on *the misery of man without God* might have encouraged in him the sin of spiritual pride, the *concupiscence de l'esprit*: and how fast a hold he has of humility![21]

But what could it mean, to follow up the dismaying catalogue of vanity, dishonesty, self-deception, insincerity, cowardice, and pettiness, with the words, 'Actually, considering that much greater maturity is required for these qualities, than for any mathematical or scientific greatness...'?

20 *Milton* (1947), p.9; the words that I have italicised are not to be found in *On Poetry and Poets*, p.154.
21 *Selected Essays*, p.414.

46

And what does this unremarked incomprehensibility suggest as to the attention with which Eliot has been not only published but read for the half of a century since the vitiated wording of *Essays Ancient and Modern* in 1936 and then of the expanded edition of *Selected Essays* in 1951?

Incomprehensible, and yet perfectly comprehensible as soon as we register all that failed to get registered when the Pascal essay was reprinted, moving from the Everyman's Library edition of *Pascal's Pensées* (1931), with its introduction by Eliot, to its corrupted text in *Essays Ancient and Modern*, and thence to *Selected Essays*. For originally the sequence of thought had made entire sense:

> . . . their cowardice, the pettiness of their real ambitions. Actually, considering that *Pascal died at the age of thirty-nine, one must be amazed at the balance and justice of his observations;* much greater maturity is required for these qualities, than for any mathematical or scientific greatness. How easily his brooding on *the misery of man without God* might have encouraged in him the sin of spiritual pride . . .[22]

How easily these slips and slippages may be perpetrated and perpetuated.

When it comes to advertent changes, I shall put forward a proposition as to clues that were in the original, but I need first to quote two formulations by Eliot that are germane. He recognized that it is often in the nature of a literary argument that there be no conclusive instances but rather a pattern of likelihoods. He saw that whereas there are indeed trains of thought and of persuasion for which it must be acknowledged that the strength of the chain is in its weakest link, there were on the other hand literary arguments that were characterized, not by having the isolable item that might be a weak link, but rather by being plaited, like a rope, not linked like a chain. Which means that a concurrence of threads or filaments may garner a strength that is something quite other than the weakness or strength of any one of the strands that cooperate in its formation.

22 My italics in the first case.

Of one scholar, Eliot wrote in a review that she 'has not quite as clear a case as Dr. Schoell had in tracing the borrowings of Chapman, but her accumulation of probabilities, powerful and concurrent, leads to conviction'.[23] Of another scholar, that he called in evidence 'many other parallels, each slight in itself, but having a cumulative plausibility'. It is these formulations, of an accumulation of probabilities and of a cumulative plausibility, that I invoke in suggesting that one persistent feature of Eliot's post-publication revision is that there will so often be found to be a word or phrase in the original text that did itself prompt the subsequent act of revision. Such a word or phrase could then act as 'a monitor to avert us', could bear witness to a 'suspicious and interrogating eye'.[24] The earlier wording, which was to prove unsatisfactory, can often be seen to invite, to bespeak, a double act of self-criticism: double, first, in that the writer is having second thoughts of a kind that must, however leniently, constitute a criticism of his own first thoughts, and next, in that an intimation of this, an incipient self-criticism, can often be found to be stirring in the original wording. Vigilance is at one with the self-reflexive, working felicitously upon what had been an infelicity – and upon what had perhaps insinuated that all was not well.

This is, in certain respects, to effect no more than an application of the insight that was unforgettably introduced by Eliot in 'Tradition and the Individual Talent' (1919):

> The existing monuments form an ideal order among themselves, which is modified by the introduction of the new (the really new) work of art among them. The existing order is complete before the new work arrives; for order to persist after the super-vention of novelty, the *whole* existing order must be, if ever so slightly, altered; and so the relations, proportions, values of each work of art toward the whole are readjusted; and this is confor-mity between the old and the new.[25]

---

23 *Inventions of the March Hare*, p.xxviii.
24 The monitor, on kinship with a dead poet: *The Egoist* (July 1919). The eye, on Sir Thomas Browne: *The Chapbook* (April 1921).
25 *Selected Essays*, p.15.

Revision is itself a readjustment that seeks to create anew a conformity between the old and the new. One figure of speech that might cooperate with that of Eliot's monuments is the family, where the introduction of the new (a new child, a new spouse, a new in-law) alters, if ever so slightly, all the existing relations.

Can there be this degree of organic congruity? Well, the artist aspires to it. Will there always, or usually, be left some sign that the reviser has been at work, some give-away, some imperfection? Not seamless but seamful? Boswell commented on Johnson's revisions of *The Lives of the Poets*:

> It is remarked by Johnson, in considering the works of a poet that 'amendments are seldom made without some token of a rent;' but I do not find that this is applicable to prose. We shall see that though his amendments in this work are for the better, there is nothing of the *pannus assutus*; the texture is uniform: and indeed, what had been there at first, is very seldom unfit to have remained.[26]

In the case of Eliot, the token of a rent is scarcely ever visible *after* a revision has been accomplished. This final wording, it comes to seem, is how the thing was always meant to be. And yet it is as though the earlier wording could not wait to be put right, as though a *prior* token had been given that there was creative work still to be done.

Two different kinds of self-reference might be in play. The first is the writer's necessarily thinking of himself or herself, and thinking too of the relation between the present self, revising away, and the past self, who set down this. The second kind of self-reference is that which is heard when something in the very words of the original constitutes an acknowledgement of self-dissatisfaction, the words ill-at-ease. Not necessarily a sound as loud as *crying out for* rectification, but tacitly inviting it. And a particular form of this may be audible when a writer is engaged in some inquiry as to exactly what the self is, or as to the multiplicities of self that might be entertained. In 'The Social Function of Poetry', Eliot was concerned to

26 *Boswell's Life of Johnson*, ed. G. Birkbeck Hill, revised L.F.Powell, iii (1934) 38.
  *pannus assutus*: patch sewn on (Horace, Art of Poetry).

understand what the more-than-social function of acquiring a foreign language is when it comes to self. That this particular undertaking should have put him under such an obligation to acquire another wording for these thoughts, that he should so thoroughly have been moved to revision, and this after publication, has its manifest aptness.

Here is the first published version of a crucial sentence:

> One of the reasons for trying to learn a foreign language well is that it gives us a kind of supplementary personality; one of the reasons for not acquiring another language to use instead of our own is that hardly anybody really wants to become a different person.[27]

And here is the later version:

> One of the reasons for learning at least one foreign language well is that we acquire a kind of supplementary personality; one of the reasons for not acquiring a new language *instead* of our own is that most of us do not want to become a different person.[28]

Or, to show the revisions one by one:

> One of the reasons for trying to learn a [> *learning at least one*] foreign language well is that it gives us [> *we acquire*] a kind of supplementary personality; one of the reasons for not acquiring another [> *a new*] language to use instead [> *instead* ITALICS] of our own is that hardly anybody really wants [> *most of us do not want*] to become a different person.

There the scrupulous revising reveals Eliot as seeking new language for his engagement with his own thinking. The re-writing is itself continuous with the question of supplementing one's personality without becoming a different person.

The provocation or clue in the original text, the planted hint that all is not well and that something may later need attention and vigilance, can take the simplest local form. The critic who has

27  *The Adelphi* (July/September 1945).
28  *On Poetry and Poets*, p. 19.

written the words *strictly speaking* may be moved to ask himself whether it was a strict, as against a laxly rhetorical, way of speaking that he had promulgated. And he may do as Eliot did: drop the two words and their self-serving coercion.[29] The scholar who makes free with an accusatory *like most scholars* may come to the conclusion that he, too, was behaving like most scholars, in not attaching his own undeveloped generalization to any sufficient evidence. So the opening sentence here had to go, leaving the succinct objectivity of one of Eliot's best formulations:

> Mr. Cruickshank, like most scholars, feels obliged to offer some undeveloped generalizations which do not attach themselves at once to his evidence. It is difficult – it is perhaps the supreme difficulty of criticism – to make the facts generalize themselves; but Mr. Cruickshank at least presents us with facts which are capable of generalization.[30]

Or there may a particular formation of which the ugliness or inadequacy is only belatedly recognized: *art-emotions*, for instance, a canting term that has no emotional reality and that was duly to find itself banished in favour of the conveying of simple 'feeling': 'blank verse within Shakespeare's lifetime . . . became the vehicle of more varied and more intense art-emotions than it has ever conveyed since.'[31]

The anonymous critical writings have their share of these self-critical prunings: the dropping, twice, of the word *peculiar* (particularly unpeculiar when repeated?) from the essay on Marston[32]; and the modification of what, in its syntactical inversion, had come to sound somewhat romantic itself: 'Conceded the utmost freedom, yet would the romantic drama remain inferior'.[33] This self-satisfied

29 Introduction to *Seneca His Tenne Tragedies* (1927), p.xii: 'The characters of Seneca's plays have no subtlety and, strictly speaking, no "private life"'. *Selected Essays*, p.70: '... and no "private life"'.
30 *Athenaeum* (11 June 1920); revised *Selected Essays*, p.205.
31 *Art & Letters* (Autumn 1919); 'feeling', *Selected Essays*, p.118.
32 *Times Literary Supplement* (26 July 1934), 'peculiar Italian', 'a peculiar Marston tone'; revised *Selected Essays*, pp.224, 227.
33 'Philip Massinger', *Times Literary Supplement* (27 May 1920); *Selected Essays*, p.214.

Paterian turn is inferior to the unaffected word-order that replaced it: '... the romantic drama would yet remain inferior'.[34]

Self-congratulation invites a subsequent self-criticism, as when Eliot catches himself playing one of the games that most tempted him: the announcement of a *few* to whom he blessedly belongs. Whereas the 'happy few' of *Henry V* were being urged to glory in their willingness to give their lives, the few invoked in Eliot are usually to be found couched in much more comfortable surroundings.[35] But Eliot showed himself, on occasion at least, alert to the temptation to which he had formerly yielded. Of Middleton, he had written:

> Yet he wrote one tragedy which more than any play except those of Shakespeare has a profound and permanent moral value and horror; and one comedy which more than any Elizabethan comedy realizes a free and noble womanhood; and he remains, inscrutable, unphilosophical, interesting only to those few who care for such things.[36]

The right ending was achieved only when, in revision, Eliot cut his protestation down to size, when he dropped the last fifteen words. For the right ending is not upon a note of self-congratulation, of exclusivity and belonging and hauteur, but with the praise of Middleton himself, and even more, with the praise of his creation, his Moll. The sense that something free and noble is being realized

---

34 Elsewhere, Eliot drops the word 'romantic', perhaps as too easily pejorative. Of Hardy: 'In consequence of his self-absorption, he makes a great deal of landscape; for romantic landscape is a passive creature which lends itself to an author's mood'. In revision: 'for landscape is...' *Virginia Quarterly Review* (January 1934); revised as *After Strange Gods* (1934), p.55.

35 National self-congratulation, the various notes of which were sounded in *Henry V*, animates a moment in the essay on Wilkie Collins and Dickens: 'In detective fiction we are inclined to assert England at present "whips the universe"'. Eliot revised this into a decent decorum ('England probably excels other countries'). It hadn't worked, the clash between the formal register of 'we are inclined to assert', and the demotic '"whips the universe"', with its inverted commas whipped into place; the factitious liveliness had come to feel whipped up. *Times Literary Supplement* (4 August 1927); revised *Selected Essays*, p.464.

36 *Times Literary Supplement* (30 June 1927); revised *Selected Essays*, p.170.

(in the criticism, by courtesy of the creation), which had been imperilled by the overstated drawl of the closing self-aggrandisement, is recovered, and the final note is of a free and noble manhood.

Sometimes it is not so much a rhetoric as a thoroughgoing judgment that Eliot feels obliged to reconsider, prompted perhaps by a faintly uneasy turn of phrase in the original. 'Such is the essence of the tragedy of *Macbeth* – the habituation to crime, the deadening of all moral sense'.[37] The over-insistence of the last six words is excised, as too summarily judging the Macbeth of the closing scenes, a man whose moral sense is not altogether dead but is in some ways painfully, newly, alive. There had been in the critic, momentarily, some deadening of the moral sense in this very determination.[38]

A judgment on a particular play, or on a particular character within a play, may widen to a judgment on dramatic language. And later, on reflection, the antithesis upon which the argument turned may come to seem coarse.

> The art of dramatic language, we must remember, is as near to oratory as to ordinary speech or to other poetry. On the stage, M. Jean Cocteau reminds us, we must weave a pattern of coarse rope that can be apprehended from the back of the pit, not a pattern of lace that can only be apprehended from the printed page. We are not entitled to try fine effects unless we achieve the coarse ones.[39]

The first and the last sentences remain; the middle one was excised, for the alternative, coarse rope versus fine lace, has come to be seen as too conveniently drastic. (Are there no worthwhile weavings that are neither of these extremes? Can the back of the pit really be reached only by consciously coarse effects?)

37 *Times Literary Supplement* (30 June 1927); revised *Selected Essays*, p.164.
38 Conversely, Farinata in Dante ceases to be judged noble: 'Proceeding through the *Inferno* on a first reading, we get a succession of phantasmagoric but clear images, of images which are coherent, in that each reinforces the last; of glimpses of individuals made memorable by a perfect phrase, like that of the proud noble Farinata degli Uberti'. On a first reading (and writing), *noble*, but not on a second writing. *Dante*, 1929, p.246; revised *Selected Essays*, p.246.
39 Introduction to *Seneca His Tenne Tragedies*, p.xxxvii; revised *Selected Essays*, p.91.

Yet no practice of self-criticism is impeccable, and there are bound to be moments when one does rather wish that Eliot had stuck to his guns instead of surrendering. Did his word 'ridiculous' too much prompt his deciding that on one occasion his judgment had been ridiculous?

> *The midwife placed her hand on his thick skull,*
> *With this prophetic blessing*: Be thou dull. . . .
>
> *A numerous host of dreaming saints succeed,*
> *Of the true old enthusiastic breed.*

This is audacious and splendid; it belongs to satire beside which Marvell's Satires are random babbling, but it is perhaps as exaggerated as:

> *Oft he seems to hide his face,*
> *But unexpectedly returns,*
> *And to his faithful champion hath in place*
> *Bore witness gloriously; whence Gaza mourns,*
> *And all that band them to resist*
> *His uncontrollable intent.*

How oddly the sharp Dantesque phrase 'whence Gaza mourns' springs out from the brilliant but ridiculous contortions of Milton's sentence![40]

I find myself wishing that Eliot had not dropped the two words 'but ridiculous' (Milton can take it), words that are themselves audacious and splendid, oddly springing out from his brilliant sentence.[41]

40 *Times Literary Supplement* (31 March 1921); revised *Selected Essays*, pp.301–2.
41 Sometimes Eliot does not cut but adds, inspiredly, to make good a claim. 'Dickens's figures belong to poetry, like figures of Dante or Shakespeare, in that a single phrase, either by them or about them, may be enough to set them wholly before us. Collins has no phrases. Dickens can with a phrase make a character as real as flesh and blood' – whereupon Eliot added, in revision, just such a phrase from Dickens: '*What a life young Bailey's was!*' This brings the praise to life. (*Times Literary Supplement*, 4 August 1927; revised *Selected Essays*, p.462.) There are occasions when the self-referential or self-reflexive word, instead of being an incitement from the original text, surfaces in revision:

The sharp clarity of 'ridiculous' is the opposite of that which Eliot most came to oppose in his earlier ways of putting things. Take the revision of 'nebula' to 'suggestiveness' in the Dryden essay when it praises 'To the Memory of Mr. Oldham': 'From the perfection of such an elegy we cannot detract; the lack of nebula is compensated by the satisfying completeness of the statement'.[42] It is not that the word 'nebula' in itself is objectionable, for in the Marvell essay it is developed, in the vicinity of 'the suggestiveness of true poetry', within a haunting comparison of Marvell and William Morris:

> The day-dreamy feeling of Morris is essentially a slight thing; Marvell takes a slight affair, the feeling of a girl for her pet, and gives it a connexion with that inexhaustible and terrible nebula of emotion which surrounds all our exact and practical passions and mingles with them.[43]

But in the Dryden essay, 'nebula' had been nebulous, slackly suggestive. Its replacement, the unromantic 'suggestiveness', then creates a steady equipollence of the two abstract nouns, suggestiveness / completeness.

What was called for, then, was scepticism about one's own phrasing, phrasing that was always better than one might have done but not always as good as it might have been. So it is not surprising that Eliot's discussion of scepticism should itself have been revisited by him, with creative scepticism, in revision. In the original account, scepticism had been characterized as

> There is, of course, a long distance separating the furibund fluency of old Hieronimo and the broken words of Lear. There is also a difference between the famous
>
> > Oh eyes no eyes, but fountains full of tears!
> > Oh life no life, but lively form of death!
>
> and the superb 'additions to Hieronimo'.

(Added to '"Rhetoric" and Poetic Drama' in *Selected Essays*, p.39.) Making a difference, the instances are themselves a superb addition.

42 *Times Literary Supplement* (9 June 1921); revised *Selected Essays*, p.316.
43 *Selected Essays*, p.300.

a habit of examining evidence, and a capacity for delayed decision. Scepticism is a highly civilized faculty, but one of which
society can die: for the abuse of scepticism is pyrrhonism. Where
scepticism is strength, pyrrhonism is weakness, the inability to
endure the strain of doubt and decision: and it is a malady from
which we suffer to-day culturally as well as in religion.[44]

On second thoughts, scepticism becomes

the habit of examining evidence and the capacity for delayed
decision. Scepticism is a highly civilised trait, though, when it
declines into pyrrhonism, it is one of which civilisation can die.
Where scepticism is strength, pyrrhonism is weakness, for we
need not only the strength to defer a decision, but the strength
to make one.[45]

It was Eliot's capacity for delayed decision, or rather for re-decision
in revision, that had come to create the humane finality of the new
close: 'for we need not only the strength to defer a decision, but the
strength to make one'. The words themselves profit from the
strength that came from a deferred decision, one among many
inspired decisions and revisions in Eliot.

Self-criticism, in those who have genius, ought to be heartening
to those of us who have no such thing. Eliot famously issued a
remark that is sometimes quoted as though it were a free-standing
declaration in itself,[46] whereas it is parenthetical (though marked,
not by lunulae, as the present parenthesis is, but by commas). Of
Aristotle:

in his short and broken treatise he provides an eternal example
– not of laws, or even of method, for there is no method except
to be very intelligent, but of intelligence itself swiftly operating
the analysis of sensation to the point of principle and definition.[47]

44 *Prospect for Christendom* (1945), ed. Maurice B. Reckitt, p.64.
45 *Notes towards the Definition of Culture*, p. 29.
46 For instance, in *The Oxford Book of Aphorisms*, ed. John Gross (1983), p.295:
   'There is no method except to be very intelligent'.
47 'The Perfect Critic', *The Sacred Wood* (1920), p.10.

William Empson, a genius, once characterized intelligence (he was not defining it, exactly) in a parenthesis, when – under the auspices of Eliot, in *The Criterion*[48] – he praised two geniuses:

> Now Aristotle himself produced the argument about parallaxes, and Copernicus over-rode it; I find this a pleasing historical fact because it shows that both these great men were more intelligent (less at the mercy of their own notions) than Mr. Burtt wishes to think them.

The notions at whose mercy a writer may be are often the notions as they were first formulated, coming perhaps easily to hand and to mind, and too easily settled for. A small revision may mean much, as when in his essay on Pascal, Eliot drops what is for him an unsympathetic word, 'liberal', from the phrase 'the modern liberal Catholic'.[49] We should not make too much of this, but Eliot made something of it in making the change, and this within an essay in which the very slightness of a writerly decision is described as proportionate to its significance: 'Yet, in the *Pensées*, at the very end of his life, we find passage after passage, and the slighter they are the more significant, almost "lifted" out of Montaigne, down to a figure of speech or a word'.[50]

What might seem two casual words, *other people*, are found to carry great weight within another religious passage that was crucially revised. In *Prospect for Christendom*, this had read:

> To believe that *we* are religious people and that the other people are without religion and must be converted, is a belief which can be endured with some complacency.[51]

The tone of this was not without a sarcastic complacency. In *Notes towards the Definition of Culture*, the substantive conclusion may seem the same, but the tone has become direct, without distortion:

48 *The Criterion*, x (October 1930) 169.
49 Introduction to *Pascal's Pensées* (1931): 'Pascal's belief in miracles, which plays a larger part in his construction than it would in that, at least, of the modern liberal Catholic'; revised *Selected Essays*, p.409.
50 *Selected Essays*, p.410.
51 *Prospect for Christendom*, p.66.

> To believe that *we* are religious people and that other people are without religion is a simplification which approaches distortion.[52]

Eliot's suspicion of any easy contrast of ourselves with other people, in the immediate vicinity of the word 'complacency', had moved him to the unmistakability of italics in *After Strange Gods*:

> Mr. Pound's Hell, for all its horrors, is a perfectly comfortable one for the modern mind to contemplate, and disturbing to no one's complacency: it is a Hell for the *other people*, the people we read about in the newspapers, not for oneself and one's friends.[53]

This contemplates the depths of tragedy. But it is characteristic of the protean nature of revision that there will be glimpses of comedy, of serious comedy, even in the religious apprehensions. As originally published, anonymously, in the *Times Literary Supplement* (16 June 1927), the essay on Machiavelli had remarked 'how the neglect of religion, occasioned by the Church of Rome, has contributed to the ruin of Italy'. Next year, in *For Lancelot Andrewes*, this had become 'occasioned by the vagaries of the Church of Rome'.[54] More centrally, less of a vagary, there had been Eliot's decision to discard two words that had constituted a crux in the essay on Archbishop Bramhall. Originally:

> Bramhall affirmed the divine right of kings: Hobbes rejected this noble but untenable faith, and asserted in effect the divine right of power, however come by.[55]

---

52 *Notes towards the Definition of Culture*, p.32.
53 *After Strange Gods*, p.43. Likewise *The Listener* (17 February 1937): 'One reason why the lot of the secular reformer or revolutionist seems to me to be the easier is this: that for the most part he conceives of the evils of the world as something external to himself. They are thought of either as completely impersonal, so that there is nothing to alter but machinery; or if there is evil *incarnate*, it is always incarnate in the *other people* – a class, a race, the politicians, the bankers, the armament makers, and so forth – never in oneself'.
54 *For Lancelot Andrewes* (1928), p.56. The essay was not included in *Selected Essays*.
55 *Theology* (July 1927), p.16.

But the central admission ceased to be admitted, and the divine right of kings became simply 'this noble faith'.[56] The caveat about it has become no longer tenable.

No less than the religious thinking, the political thinking was subjected to a new scepticism. The address on 'Catholicism and International Order' was a conjunction of religion and politics, with the political lending itself to the polemical. As originally affirmed:

> I am not denying the utility of the League of Nations either in the years of its existence or in the future when I suggest that it should have been obvious at the start that the League could never fulfil the aspirations of its founder – a Professor, not irrelevantly, of the science of government, and I believe a member of one of the dissenting sects in America.[57]

There is always something suspect about such assurances as 'not irrelevantly', since you don't ever find a persuader telling you that the point he is making is irrelevant. 'The science of government' fleers, and so does 'I believe a member of one of the dissenting sects in America', with *I believe* up to its sardonic tricks of coupling serious belief (non-sectarian) with quasi-tentativeness. Such rhetoric demeans not Woodrow Wilson alone, and Eliot came to think better of it, even if not of Wilson.[58] Nor did he hold to the strong assertion as to exactly where the weakness lay:

> I am not attacking the League, but seeking for a definition of its limitations: it can function all the better, if we recognise what these limitations are. But it would be better still if its inventor had himself seen these limitations, for what sentimentalism initiates, cynicism and intrigue can exploit. The great weakness of Woodrow Wilson was a theological weakness.[59]

56 *Selected Essays*, p.360.
57 *Christendom* (September 1933), p.175.
58 Revised *Essays Ancient and Modern*, p.124: 'I am not denying the utility of the League of Nations either in the years of its existence or in the future when I suggest that it should have been obvious at the start that the League could never fulfil the aspirations of its founders'. Finis.
59 *Christendom* (September 1933), p.176.

The final asseveration about Woodrow Wilson was cut, not because it was necessarily untrue but because it was manifestly under-described and undersubstantiated.[60] It had come on too strong, that reiteration of 'weakness'. And many of Eliot's propositions become the stronger when they are re-worded not more weakly but less insistently. Such changes may be very small, and I mean to list some of them now briskly without documentation. So 'we are simply yielding ourselves to one seductive personality after another' becomes the stronger when it does not itself simply yield to the seductions of insistence, when it becomes instead 'we may be simply yielding ourselves...' That something 'would be still more disastrous' becomes that it 'might be'. When 'due to' becomes 'aggravated by', or when 'In every essential respect' becomes 'In some respects', the process of persuasion is being respected. 'The utter meaninglessness' is less, not more, meaningful than 'the meaninglessness' that replaced it, and 'the grossest of errors' less unconvincingly in error than 'a gross error'. A tribute to the French was judged to have been too much: *for* 'has been analysed by French critics down to the finest particular', *read* 'has been analysed by French critics'. *For* 'Hobbes is crude and uncivilised in comparison', *read* 'Hobbes is crude in comparison'. (Which is less crudely emphatic.) *For* 'To the humbug of every century Machiavelli is essential', *read* '. . . has contributed' (the hyperbole of 'essential' having its own humbug).

The wish to do right by Swinburne without surrendering to him moved Eliot elsewhere to a precision of revision: the change of 'enjoy Swinburne' to 'greatly enjoy Swinburne'.

> The test is this: agreed that we do not (and I think that the present generation does not) greatly enjoy Swinburne, and agreed that (a more serious condemnation) at one period of our lives we did enjoy him and now no longer enjoy him...[61]

What we write at one period of our lives we may be moved to re-write later.

Sometimes these matters are small, often they are not. Compare this spiritual apophthegm in its two forms:

60 *Essays Ancient and Modern*, p.126.
61 *Athenaeum* (16 January 1920); revised *Selected Essays*, pp.323–4.

It is true to say that the glory of man is his capacity for salvation; it is equally true to say that his glory is his capacity for damnation.[62]

It is true to say that the glory of man is his capacity for salvation; it is also true to say that his glory is his capacity for damnation.[63]

Whereas 'equally true' was blind to presumption, 'also true' – in its modest flatness – declines to rule on the equipollence of the two truths.

Of some borrowings by Pascal from Montaigne, Eliot said (it will be remembered) 'the slighter they are the more significant'. The principle, which recognizes that for want of a nail, the shoe was lost, and so to all the larger losses, can be seen at work in, for instance, the small crucial point of speech that is the preposition.[64]

*For* 'the humour which spent its last breath on the decadent genius of Dickens', *read* 'in the . . .'.[65] *For* 'If, then, we must be very careful in applying terms of censure, like "diffuse", we must be equally careful in praise', *read* '. . . careful of praise'.[66] (Carefully differentiated, these.)

The intense feeling, ecstatic or terrible, without an object or exceeding its object, is something which every person of sensibility has known; it is doubtless a subject of study to pathologists.

Not, upon reflection, 'to pathologists' but 'for pathologists'.[67] An

---

62 Introduction to Baudelaire, *Intimate Journals* (1930).

63 *Selected Essays*, p.429. In the previous paragraph, Eliot cut out the surplusage, for instance the repetition by which 'conceive of' followed 'conception', and the flaccidity of 'to think of it'. Originally: 'Having an imperfect, vague romantic conception of Good, he was at least able to see that to conceive of the sexual act as evil is more dignified, less boring, than to think of it as the natural, "life-giving," cheery automatism of the modern world'. Revised *Selected Essays*: *for* 'see that to conceive of', *read* 'to understand that', and *for* 'than to think of it as', *read* 'than as'.

64 Eliot's prepositions are often the tacit surprises within the poems: 'The morning comes to consciousness' – not *with* but *of*, in 'Preludes II'. And the fears in 'Marina' 'Are become unsubstantial, reduced' – not *to* but '*by* a wind'.

65 *Art & Letters* (Autumn 1919); 'Christopher Marlowe', *Selected Essays*, p.123.

66 *Athenaeum* (16 January 1920); *Selected Essays*, p.324.

67 *Athenaeum* (26 September 1919); *Selected Essays*, p.146.

exactitude that might be pathological could also be a matter of spiritual accuracy, crystallized in the grain that is a preposition:

> Underneath the convention there is the stratum of permanent truth to human nature.

> Underneath the convention there is the stratum of truth permanent in human nature.[68]

Spiritual accuracy may ask historical accuracy. *For* 'the same lack of balance which is a general characteristic of the philosophers of the Renaissance', *read* '. . . characteristic of philosophers after the Renaissance'[69]. Such revisions are on the smallest of scale, but are answerable to the largest of historical claims. Such *corrigenda* bear witness to a great man's corrigibility. So I am moved by the scruple of a tiny change, again a historical nuance, within one of Eliot's most evocative tributes, to Jasper Heywood's Elizabethan translation of Seneca. ('The persons addressed are the dead children of Hercules, whom he has just slain in his madness.')

> 'Goe hurtles soules, whom mischiefe hath opprest
> Even in first porch of life but lately had,
> And fathers fury goe unhappy kind
> O litle children, by the way ful sad
>      Of journey knowen.
>   Goe see the angry kynges.'

> Nothing can be said of such a translation except that it is perfect. It is a last echo of the earlier tongue, the language of Chaucer, with an overtone of that Christian piety and pity which disappears from Elizabethan verse.[70]

Nothing can be said of such an appreciative felicity in quotation except that it is perfect. But the critical precision needed to be at one with historical precision, which is why the closing words, '. . . which disappears from Elizabethan verse', had to become '. . . which disappears with Elizabethan verse'.[71]

68 *Times Literary Supplement* (30 June 1927); *Selected Essays*, p.163.
69 'John Bramhall'. *Theology* (July 1927), p.15; *Selected Essays*, p.358.
70 Introduction to *Seneca His Tenne Tragedies* (1927), pp.liii–liv.
71 'Seneca in Elizabethan Translation', *Selected Essays*, p.104.

A healthy relation of verse to prose, or of poetry to prose, was a recurrent concern of Eliot's. Of Milton's prose, it was said that it was too near half-formed poetry to be good prose. Some of the post-publication revisions of Eliot's own prose were to ensure that there would be no feeling of half-formed poetry. This might be a matter of removing an extended flourish, a poetical conceit that is felt to have become luxururiant.

> The movement of culture would proceed in a kind of cycle as in vegetable nature, the roots imbibing nourishment from the soil, the sap rising through the stem, and the dead leaves falling to earth to feed the soil that feeds the roots.

This had been a touch too close to half-felt verse. Eliot was to reduce it to terse prose:

> The movement of culture would proceed in a kind of cycle, each class nourishing the others.[72]

Or there might be the pruning of a misguided figure of speech, such figures often being the mark of the half-formed, the poeticism. Of Tourneur:

> His phrases seem to telescope the images in his effort to say everything in the least space, the shortest time:
>
> > *Age and bare bone*
> > *Are e'er allied in action. . .*[73]

Telescope? Not the right word, because not allied to 'his effort to *say*'. What was needed, Eliot realized, was something that would co-operate with the swiftness of time and space intimated by the sequence of *in*, a sequence that is to culminate in the snatched quotation from Tourneur ('allied in action'): 'in his effort . . . in the least space, [in] the shortest time . . .' – this last *in* being elided (though its sense continues) in the need for the least space, the

72 *New English Review* (October 1945), p.501; revised *Notes towards the Definition of Culture*, p.37.
73 *Times Literary Supplement* (13 November 1930).

shortest time. The final *in*, unsaid, is contracted: '[in] the shortest time'. So the right word, as against 'telescope', is now seen to be there for the seizing: 'His phrases seem to contract the images in his effort to say everything in the least space, the shortest time'.[74]

The sensibility of the poet is alive in such prose, revised so as to become even better, and it is (unsurprisingly) in rhythmical delicacy or strength that Eliot most firmly moves his prose to become, not half-formed poetry, but fully formed prose. Two words were added at one point in revision of the Baudelaire essay. It had originally moved like this:

> Indeed, in much romantic poetry the sadness is due to the exploitation of the fact that no human relations are adequate to human desires, but also to the disbelief in any further object for human desires than that which fails to satisfy them.[75]

The two words that were later added ('being human', or rather *comma* being human *comma*) make all the difference in the world and in the world to come that is being foreshadowed:

> Indeed, in much romantic poetry the sadness is due to the exploitation of the fact that no human relations are adequate to human desires, but also to the disbelief in any further object for human desires than that which, being human, fails to satisfy them.[76]

The rhythm of the close is altogether different now, in its suspension (patience, clarification): '...the disbelief in any further object for human desires than that which, being human, fails to satisfy them'. The rhythm creates a poignancy that extirpates the possibility of any lugubrious pleasure in the bleak conclusion, whereas the earlier version had enjoyed too conclusively the smack of firm government: '. . . than that which fails to satisfy them'.

The revised rhythm proves itself more than 'adequate', it 'satisfies'. In the suspension that constitutes its delicacy, it ranks as prose with the exquisitely rhythmical moment within 'Little Gidding':

74 *Selected Essays*, p. 191.
75 Introduction to Baudelaire, *Intimate Journals* (1930).
76 *Selected Essays*, p. 428.

> See, now, they vanish,
> The faces and places, with the self which, as it could,
>      loved them,
> To become renewed, transfigured, in another pattern.

*As it could* . . . : in the moment of the Baudelaire essay, Eliot's prose, being human, had become renewed, transfigured, in another pattern.

I have been concentrating on those concentrated moments when Eliot, in post-publication revision, effects a great deal with what might look like the smallest of turns. But it would be wrong to proceed to the conclusion now without specifically acknowledging those revisions that matter for the opposite reason, that they are on a large scale.

Two examples, lest this be neglected. The first is a moment that disappeared from the literary criticism, one that is (as often) known to scholars of Eliot but not perhaps to his general readers. 'The Function of Criticism', as we have it in *Selected Essays*, goes like this:

> a critic must have a very highly developed sense of fact. This is by no means a trifling or frequent gift. And it is not one which easily wins popular commendations. The sense of fact is something very slow to develop, and its complete development means perhaps the very pinnacle of civilisation.[77]

But as originally published in *The Criterion*, the essay had included an amplification, one that begins with the words 'So important . . .':

> a critic must have a very highly developed sense of fact. This is by no means a trifling or frequent gift. And it is not one which easily wins popular commendations. So important it seems to me, that I am inclined to make one distinction between Classicism and Romanticism of this, that the romantic is deficient or undeveloped in his ability to distinguish between fact and fancy, whereas the classicist, or adult mind, is thoroughly realist – without illusions, without day-dreams, without hope, without bitterness, and with an abundant resignation. But this would be really a digression. At all events, the sense of fact is something

77 *Selected Essays*, p.31.

very slow to develop, and its complete development means perhaps the very pinnacle, or (as American newspapers say) "peak quotation" of civilisation.[78]

That last flourish (as to American newspapers) went, leaving us more sedately on 'the very pinnacle of civilisation'. More importantly, the exploratory sentence that begins with 'So important . . .' and ends with '. . . an abundant resignation' went. Eliot, thoroughly realist, resigned himself to its going. 'But this would be really a digression'. And yet a digression that remains – although it does not remain on the page of 'The Function of Criticism' in *Selected Essays* – Eliot's most passionately personal apprehension of 'one distinction between Classicism and Romanticism'.

The most striking cut that Eliot made within the philosophical and historical writing comes within the essay on Archbishop Bramhall. Eliot proceeds apace:

> The thirteenth century had the gift of philosophy, or reason; the later seventeenth century had the gift of mathematics, or science; but the period between had ceased to be rational without having learned to be scientific.

So far, so good. This sentence stands. Or rather, having appeared in *Theology* (July 1927), it stood a year later in *For Lancelot Andrewes* (p.36). But the sentence then disappeared from *Selected Essays*, as did the following elaboration of the point, which had not been retained in *For Lancelot Andrewes*:

> Three men who are typical of this interim epoch are Machiavelli, Montaigne, and Hobbes. Machiavelli is so much the greatest of these three (and in some ways so much more mediaeval) that it is a pity that he must be included with the others; but he is guilty of the same type of error. It is characteristic of all these men that their ideas are often right and sometimes profound; but that they are always one-sided and imperfect. They are therefore typical heresiarchs; for the essence of heresy is not so much the presentation of new and false notions, as the isolation and exaggeration of ideas which are true in themselves but which

78 *The Criterion*, ii (October 1923) 39–40.

require completion and compensation. Hobbes, like Machiavelli and Montaigne, did not invent errors; he merely forced certain ideas as far as they can be made to go; his great weakness was lack of balance. Such men have an historical justification, for they show us the points at which we shall arrive if we go far enough in directions in which it is not desirable to go.[79]

When the Classicism / Romanticism distinction vanished from 'The Function of Criticism', no such particular evocation was to remain elsewhere in Eliot, despite the continuing attention that he bent upon Classicism and Romanticism. The cut from the Bramhall essay is of the opposite kind: it went because Eliot was to evoke its considerations as to heresy more fully, more thoroughly, elsewhere (though never to his own thorough satisfaction, since he declined to keep *After Strange Gods* in print). The excised passage is well worth knowing, but mostly because Eliot knew better than it, and so knew better than to retain it here. The passage closes with a thought that continued to fascinate Eliot. 'They show us the points at which we shall arrive if we go far enough in directions in which it is not desirable to go'. Four years later, Eliot was to declare:

> Of course one can 'go too far' and except in directions in which we can go too far there is no interest in going at all; and only those who will risk going too far can possibly find out just how far one can go.[80]

But I should like to end, not with these large-scale decisions in revision, but by returning to a tiny substantial one, the dropping of a mere three words (mere?). The intersection is of the religious, the philosophical, and the critical. The revision is to the essay on Lancelot Andrewes, which had been published anonymously. In its original form:

79  *Theology* (July 1927), p.12. Cut from *For Lancelot Andrewes*, p.36, followed by further revision in *Selected Essays*, p.355.
80  Preface to Harry Crosby, *Transit of Venus* (1931), p.ix. As I pointed out in *T.S. Eliot and Prejudice* (p.171), this itself goes further than Eliot was later prepared to go ('but it is often true that only by going too far can we find out how far we can go'; 'The Music of Poetry', *On Poetry and Poets*, p.36).

Andrewes takes a word, a concrete statement, and derives the world from it; squeezing and squeezing the word until it yields a full juice of meaning which we should never have supposed any word to possess.[81]

Eliot must have come to see that the words 'a concrete statement' are oddly abstract there, for all the efficacy of the move from *world* to *word* (a movement elaborated in *Ash-Wednesday* V). The three words went.[82] The unpersuasive abstractness of 'a concrete statement' in the Andrewes essay might be contrasted with Eliot's feat in 'Burnt Norton', where there is an entirely unsardonic humour about the way in which the opening of 'Burnt Norton' pits the abstract against the concrete.[83] The word 'abstraction' and the word 'concrete' are both openly put before us. 'Abstraction' here:

> an abstraction
> Remaining a perpetual possibility
> Only in a world of speculation.

'Concrete' here:

> So we moved, and they, in a formal pattern,
> Along the empty alley, into the box circle,
> To look down into the drained pool.
> Dry the pool, dry concrete, brown edged,

Nothing could better bring out the difference between the abstract and the concrete than to have the abstract noun 'abstraction' in the vicinity of the most indisputably concrete sense of 'concrete'. But what is scarcely less remarkable is Eliot's having been so

81  *Times Literary Supplement* (23 September 1926). Contrast the squeezing in 'The Frontiers of Criticism' (*On Poetry and Poets*, p.113), where Eliot writes of *Interpretations* ('a series of essays by twelve of the younger English critics') that its 'method is to take a well-known poem', and 'analyze it stanza by stanza and line by line, and extract, squeeze, tease, press every drop of meaning out of it that one can. It might be called the lemon-squeezer school of criticism'. ('To study twelve poems each analysed so painstakingly is a very tiring way of passing the time.') Lancelot Andrewes is something else.

82  *Selected Essays*, pp.347–8.

83  Here I draw on *T.S.Eliot and Prejudice*, pp.256–7.

good-natured in his dealings as to remove all possibility of strife from this opposition. The contrast might be with the way in which Dr Leavis's pugnacious insistence on the 'concrete' was countered by his critics; there was F.W.Bateson's roguish question, 'What could be more abstract than Leavis's use of the word "concrete"?'

In 'The Perfect Critic', Eliot had written:

> The confused distinction which exists in most heads between 'abstract' and 'concrete' is due not so much to a manifest fact of the existence of two types of mind, an abstract and a concrete, as to the existence of another type of mind, the verbal, or philosophic.[84]

The verbal and the philosophic, like the abstract and the concrete, meet in the art of poetry and in that of criticism.

84 *The Sacred Wood* (1920), p.7.

# In the End

> Do I dare
> Disturb the universe?
> In a minute there is time
> For decisions and revisions which a minute will reverse.

How indeflectibly the word 'revisions' revises the word 'decisions' (rhyme as necessarily a kind of revision in its returning and its modifying), with the word 'revisions' then being audibly revised, or re-heard, as 'reverse'. (This, sardonically pitched against 'universe' within what are two lines of verse.) Added to which, there is the fact that the lines themselves revise some lines earlier within 'The Love Song of J.Alfred Prufrock', a revision that is not external (as the poet's working upon the poem) but internal, time past as still present within the poem's workings:

> Time for you and time for me,
> And time yet for a hundred indecisions,
> And for a hundred visions and revisions,
> Before the taking of a toast and tea.

The hold that a writer's revisions may have over our attention does have its dangers, as is evidenced by the way in which the inchoate fascinations of the *Waste Land* manuscript can sometimes be felt to supplant the fully consummated fascination of the poem proper. These days, *The Waste Land* as published in 1922 may find itself characterized as Eliot's somewhat unsuccessful attempt to write the manuscript. We might do better to give priority to the study of revision as a means, not an end, the end usually being a deeper understanding of the final work itself. The claims of process have been especially heeded of late, and this has brought some gains when it comes to understanding the genesis of works of authoritative imagination, but the product, the end-product, ought to exercise its claims too.

This section of my account, which is concerned more with endings than with beginnings or middles, gives salience to examples from Eliot's poems. But some prose instances can come first. Occasions, which by their nature are things that pass, furnished Eliot with obvious occasions for revision – an address to the Shakespeare Association, say, or to the Anglo-Catholic Summer School of Sociology. In such cases, the original beginnings, the preambular remarks, can be seen to have functioned both as a platform and as a trampoline. On the other foot, when it comes to the sense of an ending, the right occasion may be the duly sad one that is a funeral. The sadness may be healthily held in check, partly by gratitude, partly by the recognition, in a particular case, that the life that has passed was one that had been dedicated, not to sadness, but to comedy's happiness. Such was the funeral of Marie Lloyd (1870–1922), music-hall comedian. May her soul rest in peace.

> It was, I think, this capacity for expressing the soul of the people that made Marie Lloyd unique, and that made her audiences, even when they joined in the chorus, not so much hilarious as happy.

Eliot originally published his tribute to her memory in the form of a 'London Letter' in *The Dial* (December 1922). The next month, it appeared, revised, in *The Criterion*, as 'In Memoriam: Marie Lloyd', and later (as 'Marie Lloyd') in *Selected Essays*. Here, too, we find the revisionary combination that we have met before, of a necessary retrenchment (given that a new decorum has become becoming) with some apprehension of loss – not only the loss that was the genius of Marie Lloyd but the loss of aspects of Eliot's own genius that had rightly flourished in the original tribute, the 'London Letter', but that had passed with the immediate occasion of her passing. The 'London Letter' had, for instance, been the richer for its evocation of her London. On the first page of the tribute, we had been treated to an extended quotation from the public prints, attesting to the fact that, as Eliot put it, 'Marie Lloyd's funeral became a ceremony which surprised even her warmest admirers': whereupon there had followed thirty lines of details as to the funeral, the names and the wreaths, all of it burgeoning and lively. These thirty lines disappeared, within a month, in the wake of the wake. And so did another evocation of her London that had been brought home to American readers of *The Dial*, a paragraph that had given her a local habitation such as was then pertinent to the trans-Atlantic world of Prohibition, of many prohibitions:

> Marie Lloyd was of London – in fact of Hoxton – and on the stage from her earliest years. It is pleasing to know that her first act was for a Hoxton audience, when at the age of ten she organized the Fairy Bell Minstrels for the Nile Street Mission of the Band of Hope; at which she sang and acted a song entitled Throw Down the Bottle and Never Drink Again, which is said to have converted at least one member of the audience to the cause now enforced by law in America. It was similar audiences to her first audience that supported her to the last.

But the audience for these remarks of Eliot's had originally been known to be in America; with a change of audience, or rather of readership (from *The Dial* to *The Criterion*), the criteria changed. The appropriate ending found itself changed, too. The tribute had been to a profound comedian. I now must change those notes to tragic. The essay ultimately ends in *The Criterion* with what had been the penultimate prophesying in *The Dial*. Eliot has seen the future and it works havoc. The Melanesians 'are dying from pure boredom'. And then Eliot issues his death-sentence:

> When every theatre has been replaced by 100 cinemas, when every musical instrument has been replaced by 100 gramophones, when every horse has been replaced by 100 cheap motor-cars,

when electrical ingenuity has made it possible for every child to hear its bedtime stories through a wireless receiver attached to its ears,[1] when applied science has done everything possible with the materials on this earth to make life as interesting as possible, it will not be surprising if the population of the entire civilised world rapidly follows the fate of the Melanesians.

Finis. Or not altogether finis, since in 1932 Eliot appended to the very last word an impassive footnote: 'These lines were written nine years ago'. Point sharply taken, then and since.

Yet the original ending in *The Dial* had had its own pertinence, its differently chastened propriety. It had responded to the sombre tolling ('When every theatre has been replaced by 100 cinemas . . .') that evoked not only Marie Lloyd's theatre but her abstention from cinema.

> There are − thank God − no cinema records of her; she never descended to this form of money-making; it is to be regretted, however, that there is no film of her to preserve for the recollection of her admirers the perfect expressiveness of her smallest gestures.

By 1932, Eliot no longer permitted himself the words ' − thank God − '.[2] The 'London Letter' had then returned from Melanesia to London, England, where the words '. . . rapidly follows the fate of the Melanesians' had been followed by an epistolary personal note that was beautifully judged for the occasion:

> You will see that the death of Marie Lloyd has had a depressing effect, and that I am quite incapable of taking any interest in any literary events in England in the last two months, if any have taken place.

This lacks the dramatic pungency of the previous sentence, the ending that was to take its place, an ending that darkly adumbrates a bleak termination for the entire civilised world, but this original

---

1 Revised *Selected Essays* (p.459) to the more accurate but less memorable: '. . . stories from a loudspeaker, when . . .'.
2 *Selected Essays*, p.457.

ending did have its own pertinence. There is something humane in its *You* and *I*, something that constitutes a different tone in tribute to Marie Lloyd and to her refusal in life ever to have a depressing effect. A coda, the original sentence had been – a postscript to the 'London Letter', and a distinctly warm one, at once touching and rueful: '... if any have taken place'.

Thinking, again, in terms of such contrasts as might clarify the accomplishments original and revised, one might call up the revision of the ending to the *Hamlet* essay. As this stands in *Selected Essays*, it has an exemplary finality, none the less lucid for delineating a mystery:

> We should have, finally, to know something which is by hypothesis unknowable, for we assume it to be an experience which, in the manner indicated, exceeded the facts. We should have to understand things which Shakespeare did not understand himself.[3]

Understood. As the ending stood earlier, in the original book-review, it had prolonged itself for a moment or two longer, abandoning this crispness of determination, and amounting therefore to no more than a summing-up that is bent upon Shakespearean tragedy, plus a serviceable courtesy that is bent upon the book under review:

> We should have to understand things which Shakespeare did not understand himself. In the Storm in 'Lear', and in the last scene of 'Othello', Shakespeare triumphed in tearing art from the impossible: 'Hamlet' is a failure. The material proved intractable in a deeper sense than that intended by Mr. Robertson in his admirable essay.[4]

This, for all its propriety, was a much less admirable, because much less deep, ending to Eliot's sequence of thought and feeling. The revision, though, was to triumph in tearing the art of criticism from what the essay itself judged to be critically impossible.

The poetry and the drama within *Hamlet* preoccupied Eliot, as did the very relations between poetry and drama. His lecture on 'Poetry and Drama' draws to its end with a hauntingly sensitive

3 *Selected Essays*, p. 146.
4 *Athenaeum* (26 September 1919).

evocation of what it may be for works of literature to draw to an end, with a vista that opens out from what both is and is not the end of the exploration.

> This peculiar range of sensibility can be expressed by dramatic poetry, at its moments of greatest intensity. At such moments, we touch the border of those feelings which only music can express. We can never emulate music, because to arrive at the condition of music would be the annihilation of poetry, and especially of dramatic poetry. Nevertheless, I have before my eyes a kind of mirage of the perfection of verse drama, which would be a design of human action and of words, such as to present at once the two aspects of dramatic and of musical order. It seems to me that Shakespeare achieved this at least in certain scenes – even rather early, for there is the balcony scene of *Romeo and Juliet* – and that this was what he was striving towards in his late plays. To go as far in this direction as it is possible to go, without losing that contact with the ordinary everyday world with which drama must come to terms, seems to me the proper aim of dramatic poetry. For it is ultimately the function of art, in imposing a credible order upon ordinary reality, and thereby eliciting some perception of an order *in* reality, to bring us to a condition of serenity, stillness, and reconciliation; and then leave us, as Virgil left Dante, to proceed toward a region where that guide can avail us no farther.[5]

This does itself go as far in a particular direction as it is possible to go, issuing then in a sentence that proceeds from the word *ultimately* in order to end, with imaginative aptness, upon the words *no farther*: 'to bring us to a condition of serenity, stillness and reconciliation; and then leave us, as Virgil left Dante, to proceed toward a region where that guide can avail us no farther'.

In the pages that follow, I shall look not so much at 'the function of art' as at particular works of Eliot's art, particular poems, and how in the moment of their ending they may leave us to proceed toward a further region.

From his first poems to his last, Eliot had occupied his poems with thinking about ends, the many different yet related things that

5 *On Poetry and Poets*, p.87.

we may mean by an end. The woman in 'Portrait of a Lady' admits her darker cloud of unknowing within the *sotto voce* that all brackets, round or square, are pleased to intimate:

> 'I have been wondering frequently of late
> (But our beginnings never know our ends!)
> Why we have not developed into friends.'

Round brackets may hint something different from square brackets; the latter may have a touch of the editorial intervention [the ontologically different standing], while round brackets may feel (do you not find?) more like a coy enfolding. *Collected Poems 1909–1935*, in its English and American editions, made subtly discriminating use of both square brackets and round brackets within 'Portrait of a Lady'. *Collected Poems 1909–1962* changed the square brackets to round. A distinctive distinction was lost.

The prose poem 'Hysteria' concentrated its attention upon a fitting ending, in the consciousness that prose poems differ from other poems exactly in this matter of endings. The *line*-endings carry no significance in prose, no? But one does have to ask, 'no?', because it is always something of a question. The precise line-breaks in Geoffrey Hill's *Mercian Hymns* have a way of at least seeming to be potentially conveying something, even if it is only the indispensability of a shape on the page. And even accidents can have a charm, like the lineation of 'Hysteria' in *Collected Poems 1909–1935*[6] (the English edition, not the American one) that gives us this as an opening, an opening of a mouth:

> As she laughed I was aware of becoming involved in her laughter and being part of it, until her teeth were only acci-dental stars with a talent for squad-drill.

What with those teeth and that [squad-]drill, Eliot must have delighted in *dental* irrespective of the lineation, but the [acci]dental effect just might happen to help us in this matter of becoming involved in her laughter.

But the ending of any poem, prose poem or not, cannot but offer

6 And in *Collected Poems 1909–1962*.

a finality that is in some respects unaffected by a prose poem's endemic abstention from all such significances as might elsewhere be effected by line-endings. The sense and the sensuality of an ending:

> I decided that if the shaking of her breasts could be
> stopped, some of the fragments of the afternoon might be
> collected, and I concentrated my attention with careful
> subtlety to this end.

End. Eliot was never to relax such concentration of his attention with careful subtlety to these ends. He would begin with the following words the last section of the last poem that makes up *Four Quartets* :

> What we call the beginning is often the end
> And to make an end is to make a beginning.
> The end is where we start from.

So it may repay attention to look at those post-publication revisions (which are sometimes of infinite interest because infinitesimal) that Eliot made as a poem drew to its end. Take the first poem in his first book of poems. 'The Love Song of J. Alfred Prufrock' ends for us:

> We have lingered in the chambers of the sea
> By sea-girls wreathed with seaweed red and brown
> Till human voices wake us, and we drown.

As originally published in *Poetry*, this did not have a hyphen and it had a further comma:

> We have lingered in the chambers of the sea
> By seagirls wreathed with seaweed red and brown,
> Till human voices wake us, and we drown.

We can never be entirely sure that the text in *Poetry* was faithful to Eliot, but the likelihood that it was must be increased when we recall that a manuscript (probably to be dated 1912) gives these lines with the punctuation of *Poetry*, albeit with a variant:

> We have lingered in the chambers of the sea
> By seamaids wreathed with seaweed red and brown,
> Till human voices wake us, and we drown.[7]

But is a hyphen neither here nor there? 'By sea-girls wreathed with seaweed red and brown', or 'By seagirls...'? Does anything save such a consideration from being fiddle-faddle?

Yet there is, for instance, the possibility that the hyphen opens up a tiny but notable distinction between 'seagirls' (or the variant 'seamaids') and 'seaweed', a distinction that puts 'wreathed with seaweed' more clearly before us, both visually and tactilely. How tightly *sea* wreathes itself with *weed*, as against the more studied coiffure of *sea-girls*, the momentary drapery that a hyphen may assist. So that 'sea-girls wreathed' is one little sequence, and 'wreathed with seaweed', assonantally entwined, is another. And there is the rhythm, very slightly different in *sea-girls* as against *seagirls*, the gait playing its meticulous part. Eliot, whose justified confidence in his mastery of punctuation I shall be returning to, is the precisian who can do so much with a microscopic detail, including on occasion the detail that is a hyphen. 'Landscapes I. New Hampshire' opens:

> Children's voices in the orchard
> Between the blossom- and the fruit-time:

The exactly realized beauty of this moment, both within the poem and in the imagined scene, is in part a matter of that hyphen in 'blossom-'.[8] Here the essence of 'between' is incarnate in the two hyphens, both joining and separating, with the first one waiting patiently to be consummated by time: 'Between the blossom- and the fruit-time'. The tone is unmistakable and yet the minutiae are ineffable; the voice cannot say a hyphen, and the syntax of the line 'Between the blossom- and the fruit-time' is such that 'the blossom-' could well be construed or heard as 'the blossom'. The difference is miniature but substantial, since instead of the quite separated seasons ('between season and season', in the words of

7 *Inventions of the March Hare*, p.46.
8 Here I draw upon *T.S.Eliot and Prejudice*, p.213.

*Ash-Wednesday*) or manifestations (blossom and fruit), there is the seasonal continuity through 'between' in the filament trustingly thrown forward by the hyphen, 'the blossom-', waiting with patient confidence to be fulfilled in and by 'time'.

I should claim, not that the added hyphen in 'sea-girls' contributes to a feat on the scale of the exquisite moment in 'New Hampshire', but that 'New Hampshire' should make a reader sensitive to such paradoxes of scale and to such delicacies of punctuation and rhythm.

A small correction went along with a rhythmical modification when Eliot, in the last edition of the poems published in his lifetime, *Collected Poems 1909–1962* (1963), at last did right by La Rochefoucauld, who had hitherto figured as Rochefoucauld.

### The Boston Evening Transcript

> The readers of the *Boston Evening Transcript*
> Sway in the wind like a field of ripe corn.
>
> When evening quickens faintly in the street,
> Wakening the appetites of life in some
> And to others bringing the *Boston Evening Transcript*,
> I mount the steps and ring the bell, turning
> Wearily, as one would turn to nod good-bye to
>     La Rochefoucauld,
> If the street were time and he at the end of the street,
> And I say, 'Cousin Harriet, here is the *Boston Evening
>     Transcript*.'

De Tocqueville: no, Tocqueville. Rochefoucauld: no, La Rochefoucauld. The correction is called for. Courtesy demanded it.[9] The worldly Frenchman (sceptic or cynic?) continues to be stationed at the end of the line, at the end of the street (delectable in its languid comedy, the return to the prepositional phrase, picking up 'in the street' from earlier, and then curling this line back on itself: 'If the street were time and he at the end of the street': just

---

9 But *The Sacred Wood* continued to think of him as Rochefoucauld (1920, p.11; 1928, p.12; 1997, p.10).

so).[10] But he has become a very slightly different figure now, a *he* who is not a *Le* (like Le Bossu) but a *La* (like La Fontaine). A he, like the speaker, and not a she, despite (oh la la) *La*.[11] Cousin Harriet remains the woman of the house (the house that is the poem). In her Boston rectitude, she is a very different woman of the house from Grishkin from 'Whispers of Immortality',[12] who was a

---

10 'Morning at the Window' has a variation on this return to the prepositional conclusion with '... the street'. And it includes one of Eliot's most inspired post-publication revisions, from 'Hanging despondently' (*Poetry*, September 1916) to 'Sprouting despondently' (*Prufrock and Other Observations*, 1917). In 1916:

> They are rattling breakfast plates in basement kitchens,
> And along the trampled edges of the street
> I am aware of the damp souls of housemaids
> Hanging despondently at area gates.
>
> The brown waves of fog toss up to me
> Twisted faces from the bottom of the street,
> And tear from a passerby with muddy skirts
> An aimless smile that hovers in the air
> And vanishes along the level of the roofs.

'Hanging' is the end. 'Sprouting' is a newly disconcerting beginning.

11 I know, I know, I am fancying all this *la/le* business. But Wallace Stevens exercised his imagination. For instance, in 'The Plot against the Giant'.

> *Third Girl*
> Oh, la ... le pauvre!
> I shall run before him,
> With a curious puffing.
> He will bend his ear then.
> I shall whisper
> Heavenly labials in a world of gutturals.
> It will undo him.

12 A poem of which Eliot revised the end after publication. The stanza with which it ends speaks of Entities.

> The sleek Brazilian jaguar
> Does not in its arboreal gloom
> Distil so rank a feline smell
> As Grishkin in a drawing-room.

woman not of a house or of a maison, exactly ('Grishkin has a maisonnette').

Eliot's courteous correction of the name of La Rochefoucauld came within the sentence that ends the poem, a sentence that deploys the word 'end' with fulfilled dexterity: 'If the street were time and he at the end of the street'. The word 'end' even seems to invite Eliot to remember the processes of decision and indecision, with their opportunities for endless revision. It may not be a coincidence that section II of *Ash-Wednesday* (which appeared in *The Criterion*, January 1928, as 'Salutation') should combine intense reflections upon the 'end' with a subsequent necessity for revision. Four lines from 'Salutation' (italicized in the quotation that follows) were to be rescinded for *Ash-Wednesday* two years later:[13]

> Lady of silences
> Calm and distressed
> Torn and most whole
> Rose of memory
> Rose of forgetfulness
> *Spattered and worshipped*
> Exhausted and life-giving
> Worried reposeful
> The single Rose
> *With worm eaten petals*
> Is now the Garden
> Where all loves end
> Terminate torment
> Of love unsatisfied
> The greater torment
> Of love satisfied
> End of the endless
> Journey to no end

And even the Abstract Entities
Circumambulate her charm;
But our lot crawls between dry ribs
To keep our metaphysics warm.

the Abstract] *Poems* 1920; abstracter *Little Review* 1918 – *Ara Vos Prec* 1920.
our metaphysics] *Poems* 1920; its metaphysics *Little Review* 1918 – *Ara Vos Prec* 1920.
13 On this revision, see *T.S. Eliot and Prejudice*, pp.227–8.

Conclusion of all that
Is inconclusible
Speech without word and
Word of no speech
Grace to the Mother
*For the end of remembering*
*End of forgetting*
For the Garden
Where all love ends

The passage toils in the toils of the end and of the endless, the inconclusible. And it was itself found to stand in need of further decisions and revisions. Where is there an end of it?

It is as though the word 'end' were in itself enough to call to Eliot's mind a sense that creation sometimes feels incompatible with any final end. ('There is no end, but addition'.) W.B. Yeats famously contrasted prose with poetry in some such respect: 'The correction of prose, because it has no fixed laws, is endless, a poem comes right with a click like a closing box'.[14] What whispers to Eliot is something that, for the poet, is in its elusive way a continuing endlessness, a finality that has immediately to grant a caveat ('or in what . . .'):

In other words again, he is going to all that trouble, not in order to communicate with anyone, but to gain relief from acute discomfort; and when the words are finally arranged in the right way – or in what he comes to accept as the best arrangement he can find – he may experience a moment of exhaustion, of appeasement, of absolution, and of something very near annihilation, which is in itself indescribable. And then he can say to the poem: 'Go away! Find a place for yourself in a book – and don't expect *me* to take any further interest in you.'[15]

But then sometimes the poem refuses to go away, and the poet does have to take a further interest in it. There comes a decision as to revision. 'In other words again...' The words are now seen *not* to have been finally arranged in the right way, and the appeasement may even be insufficient to stave off the need for a revision involving the word 'appeasing':

14 *Letters on Poetry from W.B. Yeats to Dorothy Wellesley* (1940), p.24.
15 'The Three Voices of Poetry' (1953); *On Poetry and Poets*, p.98.

> The trilling wire in the blood
> Sings below inveterate scars
> Appeasing long forgotten wars.

In *Burnt Norton* as it originally appeared in *Collected Poems 1909–1935*: 'And reconciles forgotten wars'.

The thought of forgetting moves Eliot to remember that his duty by a poem may not have reached conclusion although he had thought that it had. On the forgotten or the long forgotten wars, we may remember the rescinding, in revision, of 'For the end of remembering / End of forgetting', in *Ash-Wednesday*, and we may notice a particular revision in Eliot's translation of St.-J. Perse's *Anabase*. On its original publication in *The Criterion* (February 1928), the first section of *Anabasis* had ended:

> Geometry hung on the veins of salt! there on my brow
> where the poem is formed, I inscribe this chant of all a
> people, a whole people, the wildest,
>> drawing to our ways the keels
>> unforgotten unforgettable.

In *Anabasis* (1930), those last two lines became one, and a very different one, too:

> drawing to our dockyards eternal keels

This, which forgot the imported 'unforgotten unforgettable', drew much closer to Perse's line of French: 'à nos chantiers tirant d'immortelles carènes!'

The American edition (1938) was to bring over the exclamation mark from Perse, in which form the line was maintained. The revisions of *Anabasis*, over a long period, furnish some of Eliot's most formal re-wordings, for instance the revision of the line that ends the first subsection within the first section: 'and the sea at morning like a pride of the spirit' (1928), revised to 'and the sea at morning like a presumption of the mind' (1930). But the revisions also include some of the most demotic (from the French). From section IV. 1930: 'the yellow town, casque'd in shade, with the girls' camiknickers hanging at the windows'. 1938: *knickerbockers*. 1949:

*drawers.* 1958: *waist cloths.* (This last is Perse's own. Note to the Third Edition of *Anabasis*, 1958: 'The alterations to the English text of this edition have been made by the author himself, and tend to make the translation more literal than in previous editions'.)

Among the most telling and least ostentatious revisions that Eliot made after publication are those to punctuation. Here he knew his powers, as he made clear in a letter (28 October 1930) that bantered Paul Elmer More.[16]

> Now I will leave out the whole body of your letter and reply to it in a week or two, and meanwhile I will merely retort to you[r] last taunt. Why, my dear More, are you so foolish as to discuss seriously with a mere ignoramus like myself questions of philosophy and theology, and then go for me on the one subject on which I know more than almost anyone living. I am quite aware that I am a minor romantic poet of about the stature of Cyril Tourneur, that I have little knowledge and no gift for abstract thought; but if there is one thing I do know, it is how to punctuate poetry.
>
> Yours ever,<br>T.S.Eliot

How to punctuate poetry meant, among so many things, a recognition of how a poem may give us pause: by manifesting a pause between the penultimate line and the ultimate one. And yet how very diverse may be the intimations that such a pause, a space on the page, may give us. I shall take a run of these, each making use of the same device (if you like), or of the same point of technique, provided we bear in mind Eliot's admonition:

> But we observe that we cannot define even the technique of verse; we cannot say at what point 'technique' begins or where it ends; and if we add to it a 'technique of feeling,' that glib phrase will carry us but little farther.[17]

As originally published in *Blast* (July 1915), 'Preludes I' settled down like this:

16 Now in the library at Princeton.
17 Preface to the 1928 edition of *The Sacred Wood*, pp.ix-x.

I.

The winter evening settles down
With smell of steaks in passage ways.
Six o'clock.
The burnt out ends of smoky days.
And now a gusty shower wraps
The grimy scraps
Of withered leaves about your feet
And newspapers from vacant lots;
The showers beat
On broken blinds and chimney-pots,
And at the corner of the street
A lonely cab horse steams and stamps.
And then the lighting of the lamps!

The *ends* again, and then in the immediate vicinity of revision: Eliot
was to add two hyphens ('burnt-out', and 'cab-horse'), and he was
to close up those 'passageways'. But it is the end of this short poem
that was to be most exactly felt anew. The exclamation mark soon
went (much better to sound under- than overwrought). But even
more to the point, the pointing, is the effect that Eliot finally left
us in *Collected Poems 1909–1962*:

And at the corner of the street
A lonely cab-horse steams and stamps.

And then the lighting of the lamps.

What change does this pause effect? For one thing, it enacts
what it is to await an *And then*. For another, in biding its time it
modifies the relation of the earlier *And now* to this *And then*, as
though steadying itself in patience. And, with its technique of feeling, it changes the feeling that is prompted by the rhyme *stamps /
lamps*. We wait a moment longer. No longer is there any chance of
the stamping of the horse's foot having the air of bringing into
existence the lighting of the lamps. The word 'stamps' becomes a
momentary end in itself, since it is not immediately succeeded by
another line. There is a feeling that the poem now proffers two

discrete endings, initially with 'stamps' and then in due course with 'lamps'.

John Donne, with a famous figure of speech, set down his sense of what it is for a poem to be shaped truly:

> And therefore it is easie to observe, that in all Metricall compositions, . . . the force of the whole piece, is for the most part left to the shutting up; the whole frame of the Poem is a beating out of a piece of gold, but the last clause is as the impression of the stamp, and that is it that makes it currant.[18]

The word 'stamps' should not be denied its right to announce something of an ending, and this means allowing it to make slightly more of an impression than had been permitted by the original punctuation, with its moving-on at once with no more than a brief period. But, on the other hand, 'stamps' does not have the right to the last word ('stamps' is always in danger of being peremptory). There will be time. 'And then the lighting of the lamps'. The close of the poem now enjoys a different lighting.[19] And this, rather as the last line of 'Rhapsody on a Windy Night' comes to enjoy, though that is not the word, a different twist. In *Blast*, the last two lines of the poem were these:

> Put your shoes at the door, sleep, prepare for life.
> The last twist of the knife.

The two lines were to become at once two and three (for the white space, say what you like, is a line):

18 Donne, *Sermons*, ed. George R. Potter and Evelyn Simpson (1953–62), vi 41.
19 Other such differences in spacing affect 'Preludes IV', which in *Blast* had no space before the line

> I am moved by fancies that are curled

and no space before the last three lines of the poem:

> Wipe your hand across your mouth, and laugh;
> The worlds revolve like ancient women
> Gathering fuel in vacant lots.

> Put your shoes at the door, sleep, prepare for life.'

> The last twist of the knife.

Differently timed, the last line now catches a different light, has a different glint. The rhyme puts itself differently at the door. The injunction 'prepare for life' proceeds, not apace, but at its own pace. Preparation is allowed time to think, and room to manoeuvre. There is a wincing away from the last twist of the knife, a small hope that to prepare for life may not have to be a preparing for death, a hope that, between the stirrup and the ground, there in that final small space, there may intervene a mercy that will stave off for ever the last horror:

> Put your shoes at the door, sleep, prepare for life.'

> The last twist of the knife.

In addition to 'Preludes I', two other poems ('Cape Ann' and 'Lines for an Old Man') were finally granted by Eliot, in *Collected Poems 1909–1962*, a space before their final line. But the movement, the movement of mind and of heart, is not the same in the different instances.

In 'Preludes I', there is something of relief in the fulfilment of an expectation, this bearing witness to a social contribution that is at once a simple service and a daily ritual.

> And at the corner of the street
> A lonely cab-horse steams and stamps.

> And then the lighting of the lamps.

Let there be the lighting of the lamps, and there was the lighting of the lamps.

In 'Lines for an Old Man', there is the introduction of a new effect so late in Eliot's life (only two years before his death in 1965), the arrival at last of time to breathe before the very last moment. And then it turns out not to feel like that at all. Feels, rather, as though all the pause did was encourage a moment of gloating before the savagery of a pounce.

## Lines for an Old Man

The tiger in the tiger-pit
Is not more irritable than I.
The whipping tail is not more still
Than when I smell the enemy
Writhing in the essential blood
Or dangling from the friendly tree.
When I lay bare the tooth of wit
The hissing over the archèd tongue
Is more affectionate than hate,
More bitter than the love of youth,
And inaccessible by the young.
Reflected from my golden eye
The dullard knows that he is mad.

Tell me if I am not glad!

I wouldn't try telling him any such thing, or indeed anything, if I
were you. Particularly now that he has come to avail himself of that
calculated pause before telling you to.[20] And how exultantly right
that exclamation mark now is, how even more right now that there
is a pause of such a kind before it, an old man not exclaiming to
you at all but to himself. I tell me.

The other poem that newly issues a penultimatum in the shape of a
space (newly in *Collected Poems 1909–1962*) is one of the 'Landscapes'.

### Cape Ann

O quick quick quick, quick hear the song-sparrow,
Swamp-sparrow, fox-sparrow, vesper-sparrow
At dawn and dusk. Follow the dance
Of the goldfinch at noon. Leave to chance
The Blackburnian warbler, the shy one. Hail
With shrill whistle the note of the quail, the bob-white
Dodging by bay-bush. Follow the feet
Of the walker, the water-thrush. Follow the flight

20 This late move by Eliot was a revision of a revision, for in its first published
version, as 'Words for an Old Man' (*New English Weekly*, 28 November 1935),
the poem did not have the last three lines at all.

Of the dancing arrow, the purple martin. Greet
In silence the bullbat. All are delectable. Sweet sweet sweet
But resign this land at the end, resign it
To its true owner, the tough one, the sea-gull.

The palaver is finished.

For it had turned out that the poem (originally published in *New Democracy*, 15 December 1935) had not been finished with, had not achieved its final finished form, back then when Eliot first released it ('Go away!').[21] What does the poem gain, when its last line goes away or at least moves away, determinedly set apart from the rest of the poem? Nothing to do with rhyme, this time, no *stamps* / *lamps* or *life* / *knife* or *mad* / *glad*. Instead, a pause for reflection and for acknowledgment, before the finality of 'finished', in the moment when the poem finishes. This, and the separation-off of anything to do with 'palaver' from all the other sounds, the bird-sounds that have been sounded in the poem and the verse-sounds themselves, the delight in obvious rhymes and unmisgiving assonances and alliterations. Then there is the provenance of the word 'palaver' itself, with its reminder of who so many of the sea-men of Cape Ann were: the Portuguese. The *Oxford English Dictionary* takes pleasure in how much has been contributed by other languages. Palaver is from the Portuguese, *palavra*, word, speech, talk.

> *Palavra* appears to have been used by Portuguese traders on the coast of Africa for a talk or colloquy with the natives (quot. 1735), to have been there picked up by English sailors (quot. 1771), and to have passed from nautical slang into colloquial use.

The coast of Africa, but then the coast of New England. Eliot's headnote to *The Dry Salvages*, when it was originally published in the *New English Weekly*, ended: "The Gloucester fishing fleet of schooners, manned by Yankees, Irish or Portuguese, has been superseded by motor trawlers".[22]

21 No space before the last line in *Collected Poems 1909–1935*.
22 In his preface to Edgar Ansel Mowrer's *This American World* (1928), Eliot specifies "the Portuguese in the fishing industry".

The land is to be resigned (resignation is urged on us), resigned to a bird that is not of land but of sea, one that is not exquisite or delicate of song but tough to the point of being raucous: 'the tough one, the sea-gull'. ('The tough one' is itself, within the poem, a call to what we have heard of the 'Blackburnian warbler, the shy one'.) Eliot is always willing to resign autonomy to one of his poems but reluctant to resign a poem simply to the past. And perhaps as we near the ending of 'Cape Ann', with 'But resign this land at the end, resign it', we might be put in mind (Eliot likes doing this, right through to the memories of earlier poems that grace 'Little Gidding') of an earlier poem about a tough one (no shy one, he), a poem that repeats the word 'resign' or rather the word RESIGN: 'Coriolan II. Difficulties of a Statesman', which ends

RESIGN RESIGN RESIGN

The political palaver will then be finished. But 'Cape Ann' stands, within Eliot's oeuvre, as both having needed, in the fullness of time, to be re-finished (in revision of its ending), and as being – even so – not done with. For 'Cape Ann' commands not a retrospect but a prospect, since in prospect there are both 'Burnt Norton' and 'Little Gidding':

O quick quick quick, quick hear the song-sparrow,

☆

Quick, said the bird, find them, find them,

☆

Quick now, here, now, always

The poem that ends Eliot's *Collected Poems 1909–1962* is one that had itself proved not to be over and done with. The two versions of it are so distinct as to constitute two poems, as is recognized by their both figuring in full within *A Concordance to the Complete Poems and Plays of T.S. Eliot* (1995)[23]. Eliot's final play,

23 Edited by J.L.Dawson, P.D.Holland and D.J.McKitterick.

*The Elder Statesman*, had appeared in 1959 with the following poem at its head:

## TO MY WIFE

*To whom I owe the leaping delight*
*That quickens my senses in our wakingtime*
*And the rhythm that governs the repose of our sleepingtime,*
   *The breathing in unison*

*Of lovers . . .*
*Who think the same thoughts without need of speech*
*And babble the same speech without need of meaning:*

*To you I dedicate this book, to return as best I can*
*With words a little part of what you have given me.*
*The words mean what they say, but some have a further*
   *meaning*
*For you and me only.*

In *Collected Poems 1909–1962*, there appears as the final poem, grouped modestly (and touchingly, I find) within 'Occasional Verses', the reconsidered lines that honour what had proved to be for Eliot a human humane relationship that went so far beyond the occasional. (Not but what he had always been a respecter of occasions.)

### A Dedication to my Wife

To whom I owe the leaping delight
That quickens my senses in our wakingtime
And the rhythm that governs the repose of our sleepingtime,
The breathing in unison

Of lovers whose bodies smell of each other
Who think the same thoughts without need of speech
And babble the same speech without need of meaning.

No peevish winter wind shall chill
No sullen tropic sun shall wither
The roses in the rose-garden which is ours and ours only

But this dedication is for others to read:
These are private words addressed to you in public.

Some of Eliot's critics have affirmed their confidence in this affir-
mation of his, most notably A.D.Moody:

> By way of the dedicatory verses with their obvious connection
> with certain passages in the play, Eliot as good as made a personal
> appearance on the stage, affirming his need to be loved by a
> woman and his joy in the liberating experience of sexual love.
> This was to come back out of the refining fire and through the
> looking-glass into the secret rose-garden – to go back on the
> poetry, and to give the last word to the human being whom the
> poet had all his life been struggling to transform and to transcend.
> It can't cancel or invalidate the poetry, which remains what it is.
> But it does establish a new frame of reference, to thus celebrate
> the union
>
> > Of lovers whose bodies smell of each other
> > Who think the same thoughts without need of speech
> > And babble the same speech without need of meaning.
>
> That subordination of 'meaning' to the natural communion of
> lovers affords a new point of view; one which may detach us
> finally from the poet's, and enable us to understand the void at
> the heart of his work – the void which, to borrow Valéry's
> image, was its source.[24]

But among critics Moody is unusually appreciative of the poem.
For both of these versions, or both of these poems if one thinks
that the revisions are so extensive as to constitute a new poem, have
been disliked and even mocked. Dr F.R.Leavis, I seem to remember,
used to make a show of having taped up the closing pages of his
copy of *Collected Poems 1909–1962* lest his eye inadvertently fall
upon a poem that seemed to him an embarrassing offence. (Not
that he was genuinely embarrassed, by this date, at Eliot's having
done something embarrassing or offensive.) And Jayme Stayer has
argued that the dedicatory poem does not valuably comprehend a

24 *Thomas Stearns Eliot: Poet* (1979), pp.267–8.

93

void but does itself constitute one. Dr Stayer judges that the poem shows that Eliot's 'relationship to his poetry audience becomes one of rejection and even scorn'. The poem, it is argued, fails at evoking, first, intimacy, then happiness, and finally 'post-coital bliss'. The case, severely put, is that 'the poem is addressed less to the "wife" than to the reader – in order to dismiss him/her as unnecessary'.[25]

Much will turn on whether you believe that the aspects of the poem that are given salience by Dr Stayer are repudiations by Eliot, as against a due insistence upon the limits of the claims that readers have any right to make of writers. For Moody, the poem cancels or invalidates nothing of the previous poetry; rather, it announces, publicly, that its own privacies are respected by itself, even though others – including devoted readers – may sometimes fail to respect them. Eliot knew that his readers were tempted to be agog and gossipy at his marriage in 1957, the much-publicized marriage of a world-famous poet, at the age of sixty-eight, to his secretary, she being thirty. There will perhaps be peevish comments, and sullen comments (there had been), keen to chill or to wither their happiness. *The Elder Statesman*? The elderly husband. And the poem's reference to the peevish and the sullen, and particularly to the 'peevish winter wind', might challenge us to lapse (if we choose to be peevish ourselves, and to lack compassionate understanding) into the traditionally sour terms of January and May, the old man and the young woman. The poem asks us just to remember, please, the world that this particular newly-married couple cannot escape, except by escape to 'the rose-garden which is ours and ours only' – for there is one such *locus amoenus*, and though it is meant to remind us of the rose-garden elsewhere in Eliot, it is not offered as supplanting those other rose-gardens that are *not* 'ours and ours only', those that had been given, enduringly, to Eliot by grace and to the world by Eliot.

Something is being acknowledged in this poem that is at once outspoken and decorous. The case is different, in these matters of public and private and publicity, when it comes to an especially beautiful dedicatory poem that Eliot knew: the poem with which

25 *T.S.Eliot Society Newsletter* (Fall 2002).

Tennyson dedicated what would prove to be his last volume, *The Death of Œnone*, published posthumously in October 1892, three weeks after his death. 'June Bracken and Heather' sets store by the month of June because it was in June (1850) that the couple had married. It speaks explicitly of Emily Tennyson's age (seventy-seven!) and implicitly of Tennyson's (eighty-one when he wrote the poem in June 1891). And the dedication is happy to say, with courteous firmness, that the book itself is offered, not to you readers, but to you, Emily, – she being rightly left unnamed within the poem and at its head. None of which would mean that, in saying such things, a poem is engaged in repudiating or scorning its readers.

*June Bracken and Heather*

TO –

There on the top of the down,
The wild heather round me and over me June's high blue,
When I looked at the bracken so bright and the heather so
    brown,
I thought to myself I would offer this book to you,
This, and my love together,
To you that are seventy-seven,
With a faith as clear as the heights of the June-blue
    heaven,
And a fancy as summer-new
As the green of the bracken amid the gloom of the heather.

This has an untroubled happiness that could not in this respect be Eliot's, for he could not have availed himself of such a figure of speech, being aware that the gloom of the heather might find itself disparagingly represented by the tattlers as his agèd state of being, with the green of the bracken as his wife's youthfulness. Hints and guesses, rather, had to form part of Eliot's offering.

Yet its being said, in the original version of Eliot's dedication,

The words mean what they say, but some have a further meaning
    For you and me only.

– why would this have to mean that readers of either the play or this poem are being scorned? Why is it not a due reminder that the rights of readers are not supreme, that the responses of readers will never be conterminous with those of the writer and of the person whom his poem addresses, and that among a writer's rights are the right to some privacy, even though a writer's privacy is necessarily paradoxical?

> But this dedication is for others to read:
> These are private words addressed to you in public.

Far from finding (as Dr Stayer does) that this is 'flatly propositional' as an ending, I find that the position that it is proposing is roundedly prepositional ('for others', 'to you'), and not evasive but elusive. Eliot had always been a poet who exercised his right to elude.

But I should like to end, not with the poem that duly came to end *Collected Poems 1909–1962*, but with Eliot's most famous ending.

It is a striking testimony to Eliot's powers of revision after publication that 'The Hollow Men' should have gone through so full a process of such revision. There appeared in *The Chapbook* (November 1924) 'Doris's Dream Songs', the third of which was to become Part III of 'The Hollow Men' ('This is the dead land'). There were then 'Three Poems' in *The Criterion* in January 1925, the first and the third of which were to become Parts II ('Eyes I dare not meet in dreams') and IV ('The eyes are not here') of 'The Hollow Men'. The title itself, 'The Hollow Men', heads the sequence that appeared in *The Dial* (March 1925), the sequence now being what would in the end become Parts I ('We are the hollow men'), II ('Eyes I dare not meet in dreams') and IV ('The eyes are not here').

Which means that the world might have been left with a poem called 'The Hollow Men' that ended like this, with the closing lines of Part IV:

> The hope only
> Of empty men.

But there remained that of which the world knew nothing but which might have been hoped for. With *Poems 1909–1925*, 'The Hollow Men' fulfilled its form, adding Part V ('*Here we go round the prickly pear*'), and thereby making possible the unforgotten unforgettable ending from which the world has long flinched and which it has long embraced:

> *This is the way the world ends*
> *This is the way the world ends*
> *This is the way the world ends*
> *Not with a bang but a whimper.*

# Index

# Index of T.S. Eliot's Writings